IN HER BOOTS

VOLUME ONE

SEXUAL ASSAULT

PREVENTION AND RECOVERY STRATEGIES

TF SASA

Task Force Sisterhood Against Sexual Assault

CONTRIBUTING AUTHORS

Colonel Janice Lembke Dombi, Army, Retired
Colonel Nancy Griego, Army, Retired
Colonel Tammy (McKenna) McClimans, Army, Retired
Major Lisa (Belcastro) Bass, Army, Retired
Major Beverly Johnson, Army, Prior Service
Command Sergeant Major Rue Mayweather, Army, Retired
Command Sergeant Major Clarence Wilson, Army, Retired
Senior Master Sergeant Jeff Willie, Air Force, Retired

ISBN 9798702375359

Published by Triumph Press

CONTENTS

FOREWORD
Major General Kendall Cox (R) U.S. Army

Simply put, this is a fantastic book and should be a must read for leaders at all levels in both the military and private sector. I was honored to be able to serve with COL (R) Dombi and MAJ (R) Bass in Iraq when we all served in the USF-I J7 and they presented this idea to me. Suffice to say at the time I wasn't sure if this was something that deserved this level of focus given the operational environment, but as I watched these two leaders negotiate with leaders at multiple levels to gain their support and help them develop this program to deliver to these forward deployed Soldiers, I was impressed beyond measure.

This manual tackles a topic that is at the forefront of today's societal issues and is timely and way overdue. The testimonies of the authors and those they served with make it clear that sexual assault and sexual harassment are serious issues within our military and society and until leaders make it a priority our Nation is at risk.

I was able to attend two of the training seminars that COL Dombi and MAJ Bass led in Iraq. At first it was extremely difficult for the younger female Soldiers to open up, especially in the presence of senior leaders. However, after watching these two leaders engage with them on a very personal level and tell their own stories, the floodgates opened, and the tears began to flow...even mine. These sessions had an immediate impact on the lives of those Soldiers who attended, as well as their leaders, who then made an effort to take this back with them to home station and keep the ball rolling.

This manual provides all the tools needed to develop a much-needed training seminar for leaders and subordinates because it truly impacts all. The authors have made it personal, and that should help the trainers use real world examples that should encourage others to tell their story. The time is now for change in how we treat one another and this manual delivers a compelling message and process to help our military and society to put an end to crimes against our fellow Soldiers and Americans, regardless of gender.

INTRODUCTION

Lisa (Belcastro) Bass, Major (R), Engineer, Army

OLD LADY

Saw an old lady walking down the street
She had a chute on her back, jump boots on her feet
I said, "Hey, lady where you going to?"
She said "US Army Airborne School"
I said "Hey, lady, you're too darn old
You oughta leave the jumpin' to the young and the bold"

Yep, that cadence is the story of my life in the military. My name is Lisa Bass and I began my Army career in the Judge Advocate Corps (JAG), a 30-year-old Private, single parent with three kids and no high school education. I received my Bachelor's Degree, went to Officer Candidate School (OCS) at 35 years old and was commissioned as an Engineer. I went to Airborne School as a grandmother and became the first female Commander in the 173rd Airborne Brigade Combat Team. I served two one-year tours in Iraq, earned my Master's Degree, and retired out of Fort Hood, TX as Chief of Troop Construction.

That seems to be the pattern of my adult life... starting things late. It's a result of beginning things too early in my teenage years. My sister would say, "we were raised in a confused household." Our mom was an alcoholic and our dad was a deacon of a Southern Baptist church in Montgomery, Alabama. I am the oldest of four, and was primarily responsible for my siblings to fill in for my mother's shortcomings. When I turned 16, I had enough. I realize now that I was the outlet for my dad's stress, trying to balance our confusing life that was spinning out of control. The fact remains, the arguments and abuse became too much to bear. My rebellious decision-making process concluded that if I could be responsible for my siblings, I could be responsible for myself without the drama. I left, quit school, got married, and had a baby. That headstrong, rebellious spirit did not get me far. By the time I was 23, I had three kids and was divorced twice.

It took about a decade and a half to figure out that I had to let go of the rebellion in my life. It consumed my every choice. As a 23-year-old single parent of three, paying bills, and taking care of my kids with no child support or welfare, there was nothing anyone could tell me.

But after my third divorce, I knew I needed help. During my chaotic young adulthood, I did manage to get my General Education Degree (GED) and a Drafting Degree, where I would draw housing and engineer plans. A pilot program was offered at Auburn University of Montgomery (AUM). It was designed to measure if a person who dropped out of high school and received a GED could be a successful college graduate. I took advantage of this opportunity and began classes. At the university, they provided guidance counselors, so I sought one out. After several sessions, I was referred to a group called Adult Children of Alcoholics. I learned that my decision-making process was reflective of an alcoholic, even though I didn't drink. I took those sessions seriously, not only to better myself, but for my children who were 6, 8, and 11.

At this point, I was homeless. I worked in a hotel as a night auditor and would block off a room from customers that I used for my children. This way, I made sure they had a place to sleep while I worked. In the mornings, I would feed them the hotel's complimentary breakfast, put them in a cab, and send them to school. The maids covered for me, as they would make up the room before the manager came in. During the day, I would catch some sleep in my car, take showers in the university gym, and attend classes.

In one of my classes, a couple of guys were attending the university on their GI Bills and were always talking about their Army adventures. I told them I had tried joining twice before, but the recruiters wouldn't let me in. The first time was because I had no education, not even the GED. The second time was because I was a single parent. My classmates told me the Army's needs are always changing, and that if I wanted to serve, then I should go back to the recruiter. So, I did! I was able to sign up and not give up custody of my children. Between my GED, Drafting Degree, and college credits, I met the educational requirements. My grandmother agreed to watch the children while I was away at Basic Training and Advance Individual Training (AIT). I gave her temporary custody for the period of my absence. All the Army needed was paperwork to "check the block" for a "GO." They did not read the fine print in the custody paperwork and overlooked the word "temporary." After Basic Training at Fort Leonardwood, MO, and AIT attendance at Fort Jackson, SC, I received orders for my first duty station, Fort Ord, CA.

My orders stated that I had dependents but did not allow for dependent travel or housing. When I confronted the Cadre about the mistake, their continued response was, "you can't have your children at your first duty station." I was desperate and in full-blown panic mode. Then this female Sergeant (SGT) from the Alabama National Guard, who was in my AIT to reclassify, approached me. She advised me not to address the issue any further with the Cadre, instead to meet her at Fort Rucker, AL, after graduating. So, I did! We met at the Personnel Servicing Battalion (PSB) on post. She approached the SGT behind the desk, gave him my orders, and said in a firm voice, "is there any reason why this Private cannot take her family to Fort Ord?"

He looked through the orders and responded that he did not see a reason and to let him call that post and find out if something was going on that we didn't know about. He hung up the phone and explained that the post was closing within a couple of years and there was no reason for me not to take my family. He immediately cut another set of orders granting me dependent travel. The female SGT then walked me over to the cash cage. (Yes, we had cash cages back then.) She handed the Soldier my orders and requested a travel advance. The Soldier took the orders and then returned with $3000 cash and counted it out to me. Afterwards, the SGT and I sat in my car, where I proceeded to cry. I had never seen that much money before in my life. The Army authorized funds to be handed to me to take care of my family, and I was amazed at this new normal. She told me I had three days to pack up my family and get to Fort Ord. I am forever grateful for this woman. This woman, SGT, and leader identified a need, reached out, and used her authority and experience to provide me a pathway for success.

I pulled my stuff out of storage, packed up a U-Haul with a tow for my car on the back, loaded the kids in the front seat with me, and hit the road. I made it to Fort Ord in three days to sign in by report date, right before midnight. I was so exhausted; I barely remembered my Social Security number. I walked in, sat my kids in the chairs and went to the desk to report. Two male SGTs were sitting there. As I began the sign-in process, one SGT asked where my husband was. I said, "no husband, SGT, just me and the kids." The SGT responded in a loud voice, "Private, do you realize you have a 5:45 formation in the morning?" I said, "OK, SGT, but what do you want me to do with them?" as I looked back at my children. Both SGTs were confused; one SGT told the other to watch my kids and then said for me to follow him. We walked over to another building where the SGT proceed to obtain temporary housing for us for 30 days. He said he would give me one day, and one day only, to get settled and figure out childcare for my children. I was able to get settled and began working at Trial Defense Service, where they had an influx of discharging recruiters for fraudulent enlistments. The attorneys I worked for questioned me on how I was able to get in the Army as a single parent without giving up custody. My response, "God opened the garage door, and we all went running through!" Because I brought no attention to myself and performed my duties to the best of my abilities, my situation was not investigated. The day my window came open for reenlistment, I was there raising my right hand. I knew the matter could not be addressed in my second term.

All those leaders' actions at the beginning of my enlistment are what gave me the foundation for a successful career. The orders that put those in-processing SGTs in a position to respond with care are the orders that the female SGT ensured I had. They all displayed outstanding leadership and what *right* looks like.

Those examples are what I tried emulating throughout my military career. However, I do not think those mimicked examples were fully magnified or valued until my second tour in Iraq during my 18th year of service.

As a Major executing Engineer duties, as a Staff Officer with III Corps, out of Fort Hood, TX, in Iraq, I sat through the daily briefs. Sexual assaults were on the rise throughout the battlefield, but it was the proposed solutions by Command that got my attention. Their immediate response to provide more lighting and ensuring we were wearing our reflective belts was not what was needed in my mind. Common sense told me that if I was wearing my reflective belt and came from behind a T-Wall, I would be more easily seen. How was that was going to protect me from being sexually assaulted?

We all had the redundant "Death by PowerPoint" training on sexual assault prevention and reporting an incident. The statistics showed that most reports were not from incidents where a predator jumps out and attacks, but where lines were crossed between two servicemembers who knew each other. In our training, the missing link was the females. Senior military female leaders mentoring the junior female servicemembers on both how to come up through the ranks and to prevent sexual assault was the missing strategy. So I went to work establishing a platform to improve confidence and develop life skills through education and camaraderie that would create a positive change in attitude and behavior. It would be a different approach to teaching and developing skills to combat sexual assault versus the "No Means No" approach, which was targeting male servicemembers. A program needed to be designed based on a woman's perspective that promotes sexual assault awareness, educates women about prevention measures and provides an additional support system to complement the normal Chain of Command approach. Establishing trust and mentorship is vital to ensuring female servicemembers are safe and taken care of.

I held an infantry position as the first female Commander in the 173rd Airborne Brigade Combat Team and there was no one for me to talk to. I didn't know if I was being handled correctly as a female servicemember. When I was in Command, I couldn't discern if the challenges I was facing were because I was a Captain being developed or if it was because I was a female. I had no one to ask. I couldn't gain insight or perspective on how to handle situations. No one had been in my position before, so there were no mentors. Recognizing this deficiency, I began a program, now known as *In Her Boots*. It is a platform for senior military women to educate, empower, and inspire the junior military female servicemembers about coming up through the ranks in a male dominated environment and to teach them sexual assault prevention strategies. Senior military women becoming mentors, arming other women by providing tools and support to improve their confidence and stand up for themselves, will ultimately reduce sexual assaults and sexual harassments in the military.

As I began developing the *In Her Boots* program, which would consist of a one-day conference with monthly meetings to follow up, more and more leadership began providing input based on what they were seeing. First Sergeants were saying to me, "hey Ma'am, can you talk to my females about this ..." and the list of things only women could talk to women about grew. Daily, I was bouncing ideas off my Engineer Sergeant Major, SGM Nathan Williams, who then spoke to his fellow SGMs. Our team began to grow with the addition of SGM Rue Mayweather, SGM Clarence Wilson, SGM Tammi Snyder, SGM Carleen Williams. When they told their female Officers, CW5 Jeanne Pace, LTC Nancy Griego, and COL Tammy Mckenna joined.

One day, COL Janice Dombi arrived in our Engineer Office. She was augmented from a unit out of San Francisco, CA. I had never worked for a female Engineer Colonel before. Usually, I was the senior military female officer in the organizations I served in. It was quite comical at times for the male servicemembers in our offices. They would yell, "ma'am" and we'd both respond, leaving them perplexed. I would tell her, "I am not used to working with another female officer!" She would reply with, "I'm not either," as we both would laugh. I sat with her to explain what I was doing in addition to my Engineer duties. As I briefed her on the *In Her Boots* program and the concept of organizing mentors which would be called *Task Force Sisterhood Against Sexual Assault* (TF SASA), she agreed that is what was needed and joined the team.

We put together a conference that we could take on the road, wherever the female servicemembers were located. We called this conference *Finding Your Voice*. Our first goal was to bring all the female servicemembers in the Baghdad, Iraq vicinity together. I sought to have an OPORD (Operations Order) published with no resolve. This different approach to combating sexual assault through prevention was not well received. I began calling around to find anyone who had publication authority. As fate would have it, it took another female servicemember who *got* the concept and agreed to publish our OPORD. Sergeant First Class Natasha McZeal not only followed through on initiating the success of the conference, but she also joined our TF SASA team.

Bottom Row, left to right: SGM Williams, MAJ (Belcastro) Bass. Second Row, left to right: SGT Alexander, SGM Snyder, SGM Wilson, LTC Griego, SGM Williams, MG Cox, COL Dombi, COL Sheimo, SGM Mayweather, CW5 Pace, SGT Duenas

Once the order was released, I was notified by my Battalion Commander's office that I need to report to him that afternoon. I immediately let COL Dombi know. She said to confirm with them that I would be there. She said that she would be going with me, but not to let them know. We arrived and were escorted by a Soldier to sit on the couch in the hallway around the corner from the hallway where the Battalion Commander's office was located. As we sat there, we notice the board in front of us which had all the standard flyers on how to report sexual assault, numbers to call, etc. I pondered and then asked COL Dombi, "what junior enlisted Soldier is going to walk down the hall of the Battalion Commander to get this information?" About that time, we heard the office door open and heavy footsteps coming down the hall. As the LTC (Lieutenant Colonel) rounded the corner with a furious look on his face, COL Dombi and I stood up. He was quickly caught off guard to see that I was escorted by a Colonel, a full bird that outranked him. He invited us into his office and proceeded to explain that the OPORD put his battalion in a position to support something he was against in the first place. Colonel Dombi discussed how the *Finding Your Voice* conference not only benefited the female services members, but the Command as well.

The fact that COL Dombi escorted me as I reported to the Battalion Commander demonstrated the need for senior military female leaders to assist in influencing a positive outcome on a needed change to serve our female servicemembers better. It takes the whole military community, including senior military male leaders that listen and are open to a different approach to combat sexual assault in the military. We worked directly for MG Kendall Cox in the J7, USF-I. His support further contributed to the success of our conferences all over the battlefield. The III CORPs Command Sergeant Major (CSM) Coleman agreed to listen to our cause. Although he could not direct the Brigade CSM's to have a conference in their area of operations, he invited me to travel the battlefield and brief the Brigade CSMs personally.

It was only a matter of time after the first *Finding Your Voice* conference that TF SASA traveled the battlefield to talk to the female servicemembers in their area of operations. We continued the conferences and held 2-hour monthly meetings that focused on a particular topic. Several female servicemembers expressed how the meetings recharged their batteries to continue for another month.

After one of the *Finding Your Voice* conferences, I received an email from a junior enlisted female Soldier. Her remarks were so profound, it sent me into tears. It was at that point I knew we were doing the right thing.

> *"Thank you so much for everything you are doing with this conference. I think it's not only an important cause but essential for the well-being of women in the military. I found our conference to be both informative and inspiring. To see so many successful, wonderful women stand up and share very personal encounters was eye-opening. I never realized how many women endure the same struggle in the military. I think this program has the potential to change the way women are viewed in the military and more importantly, how women view themselves. 'Finding Your Voice' is a fantastic slogan for what you are doing – it empowers women to make their own decisions and do the right thing. The diversity in the group is also a great thing – I felt like any female in the audience could relate to at least one woman in the conference. I would love to help spread the word and would be happy to continue to market this cause. All in all, FANTASTIC! Thank you for tapping into something that most military groups are afraid to address in such an aggressive manner. Thank you!"*

> – PFC Jennifer Brady, IMET

Our tour ended after a year, and we returned to our home stations. Most of us were from Fort Hood, TX. As I tried to reestablish the *In Her Boots* program, I was informed by one General that he "watched me go rogue in Iraq and I was not going rogue on his post." He said that our program needed to fall up under one of the established agencies. I spent a year briefing different agencies for their buy-in. With no success, I briefed the III CORPs Headquarters Command with the same amount of resistance. I served my 20 years and had started a construction company five years earlier. So, I retired in 2012.

I returned to Dallas and started my life as a Veteran. I quickly dove into building the construction company as my husband had previously been running the day to day operations while I was still on active duty. The plan was to set the company up to target government contracts. I was selected and attended the *Entrepreneurs Bootcamp for Veterans with Disabilities* (EBV) at Texas A&M. I then attended the *Veteran Women Igniting the Spirit of Entrepreneurship* (VWISE) through Syracuse University with the focus on incorporating TF SASA, LLC into a business. I love construction but my passion was the *In Her Boots* program. As I wrote the business plan for TF SASA, I began writing this book. My business plan was selected by VWISE to compete in the 2014 *Citibank Business Plan* competition. I won *Best Social Venture*. I was submitting chapters for this book to the editor with returned encouragement and positive reviews. I was on a roll!

Citi Salutes "Best Social Venture"

Within months, my husband and I approached our 10-year anniversary. A couple days later, we had an appointment in North Dallas; and in the Dallas-Fort Worth metroplex that meant 45 minutes away, if there was no traffic. The morning of the appointment, I awoke to him making me breakfast. My husband and I sat down together to eat and discuss the day's events. He said he had another appointment to run to prior and that he would meet me at the other appointment. He gave me a kiss goodbye and left. When I arrived at the appointment that afternoon, he failed to show. I called to ask where he was. His response was, "I am done!" It was near the end of the day and people were getting off work, so traffic was heavy on my drive home. By the time I made it back, he had cleared out every piece of construction equipment, computers, files, vehicles, and tools from my house. He even took my dog that I got six months before retirement. He cleared the business bank account, closed websites, and emails. I lost access to everything. Here I was, owner of a construction company and I didn't even have a hammer. My saving grace was that I never shared my military income account. That always remained in my name only. Financially, I was secure.

For decades, I had been so focused on mission, getting to retirement in the Army, and then building the business, that I missed the fact that this man had his own retirement plan in the works. In the military, if you are married to someone for 10 years, then you are entitled to their retirement pay. He missed the clause that said he had to be married to me for 10 years while I was on active duty. Texas is a community property state, so even though the retirement pay was not an issue for the military, it was identified as part of the estate to be divided. He wanted everything: my five properties that I had purchased during my active duty service to include my retirement home, the construction business with all its assets and my military retirement. I went into offensive mode. I had worked all my life to get to where I was. In preparing for court, which took a little over a year, I discovered this man had a history of being a con artist. He was on a con artist national registry. Because I started out as a Legal Specialist in JAG, I knew how to set up my case. I never fully depended on my attorney. As good as he was, this was my life at stake.

I had a truckload of tragedies happen within 30 days. Death comes in threes, and I lost my favorite aunt, my father and my daughter's dad in that short time frame. I handled the memorials and arrangements associated with each of these deaths, which took a huge physical and emotional toll. I can't believe I made it through!

My divorce court date happened just two weeks after the 30 days of loss. I didn't have time to think about all the deaths and what had transpired in that last month. I was focused on the mission at hand. The court proceedings lasted four days. More specifically, it was four days of testimony, which is unusual for a divorce court. Usually one day is enough. This was a fight to the end. I was battling for not only what I had accomplished in my life, but what my future would hold. After a long weekend awaiting the judge's decision, I received a phone call from my attorney the following Monday morning. He was in disbelief. The judge had awarded me everything except a truck, the RV with payments and the boat. I was awarded all my retirement, properties, the businesses, and a financial compensation. My ex was ordered to return all the tools, equipment, and vehicles. One truck was dropped off at the attorney's office, destroyed, and I never received my equipment, tools, or financial compensation. Then one day, I heard a loud constant noise outside my house, only to walk out and see a wrecker dropping off the RV. This is the RV he was awarded and ordered to pay for. The RV was completely gutted; he even took the catalytic converter. I immediately went back to court, for the judge to say to take it to civil court. At this point, I was done.

Although I had the victory, I felt defeated. I was emotionally exhausted and my favorite aunt was no longer here for me to cry on her shoulder. I don't think I have ever felt so alone as I did at that point. My kids were all grown and had their own lives. Thankfully my retirement covered all financial obligations, so it was not like I needed to get up and go to work to keep a roof over my head. I was not from Dallas, so I didn't know people around there. I think I was in shock and utter disbelief on how my life had turned out. This is not what I had planned. By nature, I am a planner, and an executor, with things turning out at the very least halfway decent, but this was a complete disaster. I retreated to my room, alone, with days going by without even getting out of bed. When I was young, I had fight in me to support my children, but at this point, there was nothing left to fight for. There was no mission and no purpose.... or so I thought. The depression was setting in fast and furious.

Then one day I got a call from my friend John Signorino who owns the Pop-a-Locks in El Paso, Texas and is a retired Army Warrant Officer. We attended the EBV program together at Texas A&M. We had kept in touch throughout the years, discussing business development and strategies. He began talking, and I suppose my foggy responses were the trigger to ask me, "what is going on?" I explained what I had been through in the previous months and that I did not have the energy to get out of bed. He said to me, "Soldier! Get up and put your boots back on! I am going to call you every morning, and you are going to tell me what you're going to do for the day." He continued, "then I am going to call you every night so you can tell me what you did that day." And he did! He called me every morning and every night for weeks, until I was strong enough to recognize what I still had going for me. I had my name, and my Employer Identification Number (EIN) number for my businesses. I didn't have much else to sustain my professional life, but I had those two things.

With my name and EIN, I built my construction company back up. Just as I had planned, I targeted government contracts and began winning bids and doing projects for the Corps of Engineers, VA (Veterans Affairs) and military posts. Civilian contracting was different from serving as an Engineer on active duty. Although the jobs were the same, the attitudes and bureaucracy were not. *Challenging* is the word that immediately comes to mind. When I would see young female servicemembers, I would stop, identify myself and ask, "what is your MOS? (military occupational skill)" and I'd inquire if they liked it. I would tell them my journey of starting out as a Private and retiring as a Major, and that I now own a construction company. It felt good to see them light up with newfound possibilities for their own journey in the military. Then I would hear the Contracting Officer say, "ma'am, you cannot talk to the Soldiers!"

One day I was conducting a walk through for a bid with the FAA (Federal Aviation Administration) and noticed all the males wearing baseball caps, lanyards, or T-shirts that stated they were a Veteran of a war they were involved in. I began thinking that women didn't have a way to represent how they have worn the boots too. The only thing available at the time were T-shirts with sayings like "I am a Woman Veteran; I'll kick your ass." Clearly, that phrase is something I would not wear in my business or any other workplace. It dawned on me that the boots from the *In Her Boots* logo could be turned into jewelry, jewelry which quietly conveys that women wore the boots too. *Combat Boots Jewelry* helps Woman Veterans identify each other. Unless we are in uniform, we do not know who are our Sisters-in-Arms. Since all the team members from TF SASA had retired, there was no longer a platform to address active duty female servicemember issues. I thought how if I could design the jewelry that allowed for conversations to start, then maybe the connections that need to happen in the Military Sisterhood would be sparked. Just maybe that woman wearing the jewelry would be the person someone needed to talk to, be that shoulder to cry on or the source of advice on a difficult situation. My hope is that you, the women who served our country, will wear the *Combat Boots Jewelry* with pride. I believe that the boots are the ultimate symbol of strength. My hope is that you recognize that you served your country, you served your branch, you EARNED your boots!

For the next couples of years, *Combat Boots Jewelry* is what I focused on. I drew down my construction company and began developing the jewelry line. I own all the files for the jewelry, secured manufacturing, and received three trademarks.

With all the members of TF SASA retired, we left finding solutions to the many issues to the next generation. The last decade has not improved in regards to sexual assault prevention in the military; it appears things are getting worse. One indicator is the number of Woman Veterans who are suffering from the effects of military sexual trauma. Other indicators stem from statistics, social platforms, and the media. This information infuriates me because the stories and statistics that are currently being presented could have been prevented with the execution of the *In Her Boots* program that was offered, and rejected, in 2012 at Fort Hood, Texas.

After the initial reports coming out of Fort Hood in 2020, I reached out to the members of TF SASA and, from military retirement, the members have come back together to publish this series of the *In Her Boots* books and workbooks. If our wisdom and shared experiences can help one person, then that is one less person becoming a victim. TF SASA negates the fear of retaliation, stigmatism or being ostracized. We provide complete confidentiality. We are here for you. We believe you. I pointed out in the beginning of this book that I had to learn how to let go of my rebellious behavior; I never said that I overcame my hard headedness, although I like to cite that quality as Determination and Perseverance. That is what it has taken to stand by my conviction of preventing sexual assault, and that I know TF SASA, LLC can provide through the *In Her Boots* program.

TF SASA believes that improving confidence and developing life skills through education and camaraderie creates a positive change in attitude, behavior, and the decision-making process. It is a different approach to preventing sexual assault and harassment. The *In Her Boots* series addresses issues head-on while educating, empowering, and inspiring female servicemembers on "How To Do" versus "What To Do."

These books are based on the *In Her Boots* program that supports the *Department of Defense 2019-2023 Prevention Plan of Action* and addresses the elements of the *Prevention System of Human Resources, Collaborative Relationships, and Infrastructure.* We hope that this book of shared knowledge and experiences consoles, cheers, encourages, and strengthens you. Our goal is that the information and techniques you receive become a revelation that touches the heart and sparks the mind, producing a perfect alignment. By applying new skillsets, you are set up for success both, on and off active duty.

Disclaimer: *This is not a "dessert book" with subjects sugar-coated. This is the meat, potatoes, and vegetables you do not like. The truth can be bitter and sometimes hard to digest. However, growth happens when you are challenged.*

TF SASA, LLC

Owners & Authors

JANICE LEMBKE DOMBI

Colonel (Retired) served 33 years as an enlisted Soldier and Commissioned Officer in the US Army. She was the first woman to command a Division in the US Army Corps of Engineers (USACE). Janice also commanded: a USACE Far East District, Republic of Korea; the 536th Engineer Combat Battalion (Heavy), Republic of Panama; and 864th Engineer Combat Battalion (Heavy), Washington State. She was an Associate Professor of History at the USMA, West Point, and Branch Chief of Iraqi Engineer Development, Baghdad. During her combat tour in Iraq, she became one of the original founding members of TF SASA. Janice is an Academy Fellow with the Society of American Military Engineers and has four Masters of Arts degrees. She the Co-owner of J. Dombi2 Consulting, LLC and TF SASA, LLC. www.JDombi2Consulting.com

LISA (BELCASTRO) BASS

Major, (Retired), served over 20 years, seven years in the enlisted and commissioned in the U.S. Army Corps of Engineers. Lisa began her career in the Army as a 30-year-old Private in the JAG Corps. She attended Officer Candidate School and was commissioned as an Engineer. As a grandmother, she attended Airborne School and became the first female Commander in the 173rd Airborne Brigade Combat Team. Lisa served two one-year tours in Iraq as an engineer. Her last duty in the Army was Chief of Troop Construction for Fort Hood, TX.

Lisa is married to her biggest supporter and has four children, and 15 grandchildren that hold her heart. Lisa holds an Associate Degree in Drafting, a Bachelor's Degree in Government from the University of Central Texas, and a Master's Degree in Public Policy and Administration from the University of Missouri, St. Louis. She also holds Master Certificates for Commercial and Government Contracting from Villanova University. Lisa is a graduate of the *Entrepreneur's Bootcamp for Veteran's with Disabilities (EBV)* from Texas A&M, and a graduate of the *Veteran Women Igniting the Spirit of Entrepreneurship (VWISE)* from Syracuse University. She was selected and completed the *Count Me In* program for business development and won Citi Bank's "Best Social Venture" business competition for her *In Her Boots* program.

A resident of Dallas since her retirement from the Army in 2012, Lisa has served on the Board of Directors for the Grand Prairie Chamber of Commerce and Co-chaired the Grand Prairie Economic Development Committee. As the Executive Director for Chamber Development of the Dallas-Fort Worth, United States Veteran Chamber of Commerce, she provided the foundation for "vetrepreneurs" to succeed. Lisa is the owner of *Combat Boots Jewelry, LLC* and holds three trademarks for her designs. The Combat Boots Jewelry can be found at www.combatbootsjewelry.com. She is the Founder and Co-owner of TF SASA, *In Her Boots* program aimed at Sexual Assault Prevention and Recovery Strategies in the military.

Contributing Authors

TAMMY MCKENNA MCCLIMANS

Colonel (Retired) served 37 years. She entered the Army after high school as a Private. She served for nine and half years as an enlisted Soldier and retired in 2015. She was commissioned through Officer Candidate School as a Nuclear Biological Chemical (NBC) Officer. Tammy has served in two deployments. First in support of Operation Desert Storm and then in support of Operation Iraqi Freedom as an Operations Staff Officer. During her military career, Tammy commanded two companies, an Airborne unit out of Fort Bragg and a Recruiting unit in Greenville, NC. Her most enjoyable assignment was as a Battalion Commander in Germany. She obtained her degree through the Army's Tutition Assistance Program, taking most of her classes at night and weeknds, culminating in a Bachelor's Degree from Jacksonville State University, Alabama in Psychology with a Minor in Sociology. During her second combat tour in Iraq, Tammy became one of the original founding members of TF SASA. She is currently working as a Defense Contractor supporting the Defense Threat Reduction Agency at Ft. Belvoir, VA.

NANCY GRIEGO

Colonel, (Retired) served in the United States Army Reserves for 30 years in the Nurse Corps and Civil Affairs. She is one of the founding members of TF SASA, bringing her expertise as a Sexual Assault Examiner Nurse (SANE). Nancy has served in four deployments to include Landstuhl Germany in support of Operation Joint Endeavor; Iraq in support of Operation Iraqi Freedom; Operation New Dawn, and Operation Unified Response during the Haiti Earthquake. She was a commander for the 418 Civil Affairs Battalion CO A (Tactical), 172 Medical Multifunctional Battalion, 7306 MESB. Nancy was a G3 MOB Officer for USACAPOC at Fort Bragg, NC, deploying Civil Affairs and Psychological US Army Reserve Units in 2005. She was a contract employee and on active duty at Center for Army Lessons Learned (CALL), Ft Leavenworth, KS for 5 years. While at CALL Nancy was deployed to collect Lesson Learned from Operation Unified Response.

Nancy has a daughter and son, daughter-in-law and four grandchildren. She graduated from Amarillo College with an Associate Degree in Nursing in 1982. She holds a Bachelor's Degree in Nursing from West Texas A&M. She completed her Master's Degree in Christian Ministries from Liberty University. Nancy completed the Sexual Assault Nurse Examiner Course and is a certified Legal Nurse Consultant. She recently completed her certification in Culinary Arts and Pastry Arts from Auguste Escoffier School of Culinary Art. After retiring, Nancy decided she would raise Katahdin Sheep on her 15-acre homestead.

BEVERLY D. JOHNSON

USMA 1986, Major, served over 16 years (active and reserve) as an Officer in the U.S. Army Corps of Engineers. She served in Virginia, Missouri, Europe, and the Hawaiian Islands. Beverly is an entrepreneur, and the owner of BDJ Wealth Management, an Independent Registered Investment Advisor Firm with the fiduciary responsibility to serve the best interests of her clients. Prior to her current role, she has spent twenty years of her career in the private industry with two fortune 100 companies, and as an educator in a major university. Her education includes a B.S. in Mechanical Engineering, U.S. Military Academy, an M.S. in Engineering Management, Missouri University of Science and Technology, an Executive M.B.A. Kellogg Graduate School of Management, Northwestern University, and an M.S. in Personal Financial Planning Texas Tech University. Beverly is passionate about empowering, educating, and advising women on their **you**nique financial needs, and goals. www.w2woman.com Although she specializes in serving the needs of women and business owners, she also works with individuals and families.

RUE J. MAYWEATHER

Command Sergeant Major, (Retired) served in the Army for over 36 years in the Adjutant General Corps, and taught as a Legal Specialist Instructor in the Judge Advocate General Corps for 9 years. She and served 17 years in law enforcement. Rue was selected as the first female Sergeant Major and first African American female in the 4th Brigade, 95th Division. She was selected as the first female Command Sergeant Major and also the first African American female with the 94th Combat Support Hospital, 807th Medical Command. During her combat tour in Iraq, as a Red Team Analyst, she worked directly under the leadership of both former President Barack Obama and former General Lloyd Austin. Rue became one of the original founding members of TF SASA. She loves spending time with her son, grandchildren, family and friends. Rue is one of the great voices of our times, captivating audiences and readers with her fluid imagination through her work of fiction. To her credit, Yahoo Finance has recognized her as an author to watch for in 2021! She guides you in your astounding gifts Rare, Unique, and Essential (RUE) to impact the world. She leverages your strengths and shores up your weaknesses to embrace Emotional Intelligence. Rue is an important role model for many women breaking barriers, yet still remains humble. Her books can be found at www.ruemayweather.com.

CLARENCE WILSON

Sergeant Major (Retired) served in the Army for over 24 years in the Chemical Corps. Clarence grew up in Mayesville, South Carolina where he met and married his high school sweetheart. He has been married for over 30 years. They have three children and eleven grandchildren he absolutely adores. Clarence demonstrated superb professionalism, management skills and leadership abilities while serving the Army in several key assignments: RDTE NCO in the US Army Operational Test Command. Clarence became the first Non-commissioned Officer selected by the Director to become a ATEC Systems Team member; Senior Drill Instructor with Foxtrot Company and First Sergeant for Delta Company, both with the 82D CM BN FLW, Missouri; CBRN Operations NCOIC assigned to the 3RD Armored Cavalry Regiment, FT Hood, TX; EUSA Force Protection SGM assigned to The Eighth United States Army, Yongsan, Korea; to conclude an exceptional military career, Clarence returned to FT Hood, TX and deployed to Operation Iraqi Freedom/ New Dawn with the III Corps Force Protection Cell. During his combat tour in Iraq, he became one of the original founding members of TF SASA. Clarence is presently employed with Solution One Industries Inc as a Programs Analyst II.

JEFF WILLIE

Senior Master Sergeant (Retired) served in the United States Air Force for over 25 years in the Security Police Corps. He held key leadership roles as a Combat Security Police Instructor, Special Weapons and Tactics Instructor (SWAT), Non-commissioned Officer in Charge Security Police Quality Control, Superintendent Security Police Operations, First Sergeant, and Superintendent of the largest Department of Defense Joint Service Honor Guard located outside of Washington D.C. November 1983, after Operation Urgent Fury (Grenada), then Staff Sergeant Willie had the distinct privilege of being recognized by President Reagan & First Lady Nancy Reagan honoring military men and women responsible for rescuing the students at Saint George Medical School.

Only a few are chosen and less can attend, Air Force Staff Sergeant Willie attended Army Infantry School and Army Pre-Ranger School. While active-duty Air Force, Staff Sergeant Willie became a Certified Arkansas Law Enforcement Instructor specializing in Special Weapons and Tactics (SWAT) and an Honorary Colonel in the Arkansas State Police. After transitioning from the Air Force in November 2002, January 2003 Jeff Willie became Professor Jeff, Associate Faculty for the University of Phoenix facilitating undergraduate leadership, business, and humanities classes. Jeff is also CEO of Jeff Willie Leadership, www.jeffwillie.com, Executive Director with the John

Maxwell Team, International Certified Executive Leadership Consultant, Executive Coach, Trainer, Keynote & Motivational Speaker, Conflict Resolution Trainer, DISC Behavior Analysis Consultant, Diversity and Inclusion Trainer and an Educational Consultant. Jeff travels nationally and internationally (in-person and virtually) speaking and facilitating leadership seminars and workshops. Jeff's motto: "Serving and Adding Value to People, People are his Business."

PREVENTION

REDUCING THE LEARNING CURVE

Janice Lembke Dombi, Colonel (R), Engineer, Army

A lot of people have gone further than they thought they could because someone else thought they could.

-Unknown

Imagine a foreign enemy attacking between 19,000 and 34,000 United States military servicemembers every year, over the past several years, and paralyzing thousands of units in the process. Would the US military counter-attack with PowerPoint slides and fun runs? No. The military would arm members with every tactic, technique, procedure, and weapon available in the arsenal. The unit leadership would bring in experts that fought the enemy and survived. They would learn how servicemembers evaded the enemy. They would ask survivors how they escaped the enemy's grasp. Everyone, down to the small unit level, would study lessons learned and conduct hands-on field exercises to reduce the learning curve, so the same devastation does not happen the next year.

Sexual assault and sexual harassment (SA/SH) are evils attacking and eroding the US military from within the ranks. Each year the US Department of Defense (DOD) provides Congress with an *Annual Report on Sexual Assault in the military*. In a baseline survey in 1984, servicemembers reported over 34,000 assaults. Over the next 34 years, the numbers reported in the *Annual Report to Congress* slowly decreased to a low, in 2016, of 14,900. In 2018 the numbers again rose to 20,500. The current efforts to change the military culture are too slow to protect the mental and physical health of servicemembers. Preventing sexual assault and sexual harassment is not only an issue of taking care of people, but in the military, maintaining unit readiness is also at stake. Something must change. That change is *Reducing the Learning Curve*.

Despite all the revised and new programs that are rolled out every year, sexual assault and harassment continue to plague the military. Sexual assault and sexual harassment happens to people of all ages and genders, but numerous military and civilian studies report attacks on people ages 17-24 as the most common demographic. What happens at age 25 that reduces the likelihood of being the target of SA/SH predators? By 25, servicemembers increasingly find their voice. Finding your voice means having the confidence to stand up for yourself when you don't agree with something that is happening or you are not being treated with dignity and respect. When you have been in the military six years or so, you've been through the school of hard knocks, developed greater confidence, and understand the system better. It is more difficult for a predator to groom you for an attack. The authors of this book want to use our military experience of being "In Her Boots" to help you age, emotionally, to reduce your time in the school of hard knocks – reduce your learning curve as though you have been in the military several years. We will help you find your voice sooner than you can on your own. This maturity will help you in all aspects of your life as you confidently make your needs understood and reduce wasted time spent trying to figure important concepts out for yourself.

In the military, both men and women attend mandatory sexual assault prevention training. The training usually consists of a junior leader, only a couple of years older than the group, flipping through a massive stack of mandatory PowerPoint slides. Most servicemembers distance themselves from the topic, believing sexual assault will never happen to them. Much of the class time focuses on sexual harassment and assault reporting procedures, which are important. But instead of talking about lessons learned from actual cases, people argue this criminal behavior isn't going on in their unit, with many concluding that most harassment and assault reports are false. The discussion usually drifts to accusations that women are sleeping their way to the top. This is always followed by a discussion on how unfair the physical readiness test standards are because of the different standards for men and women.

You know the discussion. You've sat thru many of these mandatory classes. The required PowerPoint presentations seldom accurately depict situations that isolate victims and make them prey. Many people believe unknown attackers just jump out from behind a bush in a dark parking lot to attack women. When there was a big spike in sexual assaults at our compound in Iraq, well-meaning but ill-informed senior leaders told the women to travel in groups, wear our reflective belts, and to walk in well-lighted areas. According to the annual reports to Congress, approximately 65-85 percent of the sexually assaulted servicemembers did know their attackers, with 65 percent of the accused being peers. The attackers are not jumping out from behind bushes; they are people you know, many of which are invited into your dorm or barracks, or hotel room, or you willingly go with them. In 64 percent of the sexual assault cases, alcohol is involved. Just because you invite someone in your room to watch TV or play video games, does not mean you want to have sex with them. This is where culture change is too slow to protect you. You need to use the skills of a more mature woman and protect yourself.

Sexual assault is _never_ the victim's fault, but this fact will not protect you or prevent SA/SH. Knowing the assault is not your fault does not mean a careful person can ignore their surroundings or situation either. Very few people will talk _defense_ in discussing sexual assault and return to the argument that it is the predators' responsibility to change. The predator is indeed in the wrong, but we have been waiting a lifetime for the military's culture to evolve to one of treating everyone with dignity and respect. We have been waiting a lifetime, and still, each year, tens of thousands of US servicemembers are assaulted. We need to have a greater role in protecting ourselves and preventing sexual assault as the military's climate slowly changes.

Why is SA/SH prevention a taboo subject when it involves developing life skills for prevention? Prevention is not taboo in other areas of our daily lives. We wear seat belts when we drive, and we lock our doors at night before we go to bed—to be safe. We tuck our necklace in our shirt and don't wear flashy jewelry when we ride the subway. We build prevention into our lives every day without a second thought, but that doesn't mean it's our fault if something bad happens to us. If someone rear-ends our car, we were wearing our seatbelt to avoid hitting the windshield. Our airbag may deploy in an accident, but that is also a preventive measure, and it is not linked to a fault. Prevention doesn't admit guilt or blame. In the case of SA/SH, prevention saves years of hard work recovering from the mental and possible physical anguish following a sexual assault or from years of suffering and the frustration from not being taken seriously in the workplace with repeated sexual harassment.

When the military successfully addresses a problem, it incorporates hands-on skills training. When marksmanship qualification faltered, the military responded with additional training and drills. In the Army case, Soldiers went to the range twice a year, instead of once a year, to qualify with their individual weapons. When the Army concentrated on reducing off-duty accidents, there was a specific chart that everyone learned how to use to evaluate and mitigate risks. All the services have a similar accident prevention program; the Air Force counts on their wingmen to help them with their off-duty behavior. In the case of the Army, everyone learned how to physically complete the chart. If they wanted to go on leave or travel on a pass, even privates used this chart. Women need hands-on training from people with personal experience who can quickly establish credibility and provide the skills and training required to find their voice. Each individual servicewoman needs to be the first and the strongest line of defense against sexual assault. Not because it's her fault, but because she is the one that has to live with the aftermath of the military sexual trauma.

Not all servicemembers are sexually assaulted, and some are attacked multiple times. Imagine someone gave you a crystal ball, and you could look in the future. If you saw a predator coming, you would be more prepared to find your voice and respond confidently. Our goal is to help you look into that crystal ball. The most vigorous preventive measures will empower, educate, and inspire you with resiliency to protect yourself and do better at whatever task you attempt. You will perform your military duties better, be a valued team member, and rely on the resources already in the military's inventory to accomplish the task.

Unwanted sexual contact is not a unique military problem. According to the Department of Defense's statistics in the *DOD Annual Report,* 30% of women and 6% of men reported experiencing sexual assault before entering the military. The report says that servicemembers who were previously assaulted, either as a civilian or in the military, were 33% more likely to be assaulted again in the military. While sexual assault is not unique to the military, it is potentially more prevalent because of the number of men in comparison to women and the transient nature of the organization. A variety of factors contribute to the high number of assaults, but most can be resolved with the same solution: improving women's confidence. Some of the problems that contribute to the issue include a civilian education system that does not promote confidence, significantly reduced numbers of two-parent homes which are needed to develop family socialization, and less mature military leaders that were promoted quickly to meet war-time requirements. Make the decision to be your own first line of defense against sexual assault and sexual harassment. You have waited long enough for the culture to change. You have suffered long enough.

The authors of this book intend to share information that will not always be popular. It will rub you the wrong way. It is like eating your brussels sprouts. They are not always your first choice, but you know it is good for you. We want to be the mentors to help reduce your learning curve. We want you to thrive, not just survive your tour of duty in the military.

WHY?

Lisa Bass, Major (R), Engineer, Army

Alone We Can Do So Little; Together We Can Do So Much.

-Helen Keller

Regardless of how much one attempts to execute prevention measures, they are not 100% fail-proof. Prevention strategies learned reduce the chance of becoming a victim, but the fact of the matter is, there are evil and sick people in this world, and God forbid you cross paths with one of them. Military Sexual Trauma (MST) is the term used by the Department of Veterans Affairs (VA) to refer to sexual assault experiences or repeated, threatening sexual harassment that a Veteran experienced while a person was in the military. The definition of MST comes from Federal Law (Title 38 US Code 1720D). It is a psychological trauma resulting from a physical assault of a sexual nature, a battery of a sexual nature, or sexual harassment, which occurred while the Veteran served on active duty, active duty for training, or inactive duty training. Sexual harassment is further defined as "repeated, unsolicited verbal or physical contact of a sexual nature which is threatening in character." The behavior may include physical force, threats of negative consequences, implied promotions, promises of favored treatment, or intoxication of either perpetrator or victim. Other events that may be categorized as MST may include unwanted sexual contact, threatening offensive remarks, and unwelcome sexual advances. Military Sexual Trauma is one of premeditation, power, and control, and human targets tend to be perceived as powerless and vulnerable.

Military Sexual Trauma can apply if you are married or in a relationship with someone in the military. According to the VA, intimate partner violence (IPV) is defined as actual or threatened emotional, physical, or sexual abuse or stalking behavior by an intimate partner. It may happen once or be a pattern of events that gets worse over time. Intimate partner violence may occur with a current or former boyfriend, girlfriend, or spouse of any sex or gender. Partners do not have to have sex or live in the same place. Both women and men can experience it.

One area of trauma young servicemembers do not recognize until they leave active duty is the impacts of inappropriate Senior-Subordinate relations. This indeed falls into the category of MST. The sad thing is that many Woman Veterans have an MST story to tell, and often they stem from these inappropriate relationships.

Let me introduce you to SPC Jane (Specialist, E4), a young, naïve girl in her early 20's growing into womanhood. The NCOIC (Non-Commissioned Officer in charge) of her section was SFC Joe (Sergeant First Class, E7), a man in his 30's, who had been in the Army for over 16 years. While deployed, SFC Joe began pursuing SPC Jane. It started out appearing like mentorship and professional development. It was innocent at first, such as the occasional lunch and dinner together with others in the section at the mess hall. As the deployment became more of a routine, feeling like Ground Hog's Day, they began dining alone together. Their level of communication grew more in-depth, and a sexual relationship began. Their secret rendezvous would consist of sneaking out to the vehicles that were parked out of the sight of satellites hovering overhead. Who do you suppose had that type of intel, the SPC, or SFC? As time went by, he would insist she perform oral sex before intercourse.

For many months this continued, and as the deployment was drawing near the end, SFC Joe informed SPC Jane that he was married and in love with his wife, and that their relationship could not continue once they returned to the home station. Devastated and heartbroken, SPC

Jane realized that SFC Joe essentially used her for his pleasure. She went to her Chain of Command and reported that SFC Joe had raped her. The Command took all the correct steps by following the procedures and notifying CID (Criminal Investigation Division). The CID investigator was a female NCO who was very sharp. She did not let herself become emotionally involved and focused on the facts presented. She reported that she had a gut feeling that there was more to the story and continued to follow her instincts, proceeding with a comprehensive investigation. The SPC was so emotionally broken up and falling apart; she was in the Chaplain's office daily. As SFC Joe prepared his defense, he had his wife calling from home station, explaining to the Command that he was a good husband and a good father. His military career was the most important thing to him and that he would not do anything to jeopardize it.

After weeks of investigating, The CID team identified satellite footage and could see that SFC Joe and SPC Jane were going to vehicles at night on several occasions. SFC Joe became complacent in his strategic effort to avoid the satellites. The female CID investigator began putting pressure on SPC Jane to reveal the nature of the relationship. As SPC Jane had secluded herself to solitary confinement at this point, and after many meetings with the Chaplain, she broke and revealed the actual circumstances behind the rape allegation. The conclusion from the CID's investigation and the Command's perspective was that this is not a case of rape but a case of adultery. Both received an Article 15, reduced rank, and forfeiture of pay.

Who knows what may have happened with their careers, but their reputation was scarred. The sad thing is that although physical rape was not substantiated, SPC Jane did not possess the maturity level at her young age to process the emotional event of being rejected by her lover and leader. Confused over her broken heart, rejection, and lack of self-respect, the pain drove her to retaliate against the SFC. The means available was to report him, ignorant of the possible outcome, as she too was held responsible for the consequence of her actions.

Since this incident, all Service Branches have taken great strides through Command policy that establishes the relationships between different ranks. Army regulation, AR 600-20, paragraph 4-14c, sets forth the prohibiting of intimate or personal relationships between the ranks of

Corporal through Command Sergeants Major (E5-E9, CPL included) and junior enlisted servicemembers (E1-E4). Intimate relationships between officer ranks and enlisted ranks are forbidden, punishable in accordance with the UCMJ (United Code of Military Justice), Article 134, Fraternization. These policies and laws are in place to maintain the good order and discipline of our military. Although all these policies and laws deter against prohibited relationships, Woman Veterans continue to report how they were sexually traumatized by their leaders.

Where the lines blur....

From a sociological perspective, women in the generation born after 1980, also known as Millennials, approach relationships differently than the older generation. Traditional relationship rules do not apply for the most part and they are more accepting when things don't work out between two people. It is a generation where having divorced parents is not uncommon. So, psychologically, they are not prepared to be manipulated by a predator, camouflaged as a military leader. From the first entry of the military, we are taught about respecting the rank. A leader's rank can be threatening and mesmerizing at the same time for a young woman just coming into the military. Statics show that the most vulnerable age to be sexually harassed or assaulted is between 18-24.

The Department of Defense clarifies misuse of position to include inducing or coercing another person to provide any benefit to you or anyone with whom you are affiliated. Dr. Marion Sherman, the Director of Mental Health at the VA Medical Center in Loma Linda, California, has identified that sexual assault is prevalent among women patients. "I'm struck by the number of women who say they were pressed to have sex." Sherman said, "It gets very hard to untangle. Much of it is dealing with issues of betrayal. They went to serve their country, and did what they were asked to do, but were violated. They feel betrayed by their comrades and Commanders. They tell me they are mad at their country, yet they love that country. If you add in there some traumatic brain injury and PTSD, you can see why people say, 'I'm just going to have a drink because nothing can help me,' and it's not true because we have effective treatment." A horrible reality in the aftermath is that our sisters-in-arms decide to suffer in silence and not to seek out assistance in the recovery process once they have left the military.

If a victim is "suffering in silence" while on active duty, the "mission" will temporarily keep them distracted. There is the occasional solitary confinement in the evenings or weekends, where the silent tears are collected, but for the most part she has a mental escape from the negative thoughts and self-destruction, as she still shows up for PT and executes her duties. This is not the case for a female who chooses to leave active duty, without reporting or seeking help. These women are now living in the civilian world, often not recognizing they are a Veteran with access to resources. I meet female Veterans in rural areas that have served several combat tours in Iraq or Afghanistan. They left the military either through an elective or non-elective process and don't know they are entitled to the VA's benefits because they received a General Discharge. This statement holds primarily true for female Veterans that served in the lower ranks.

The question should be, "why did they get a General Discharge?" The answer is often that coping mechanisms used to cover the event's pain has negative consequences that impact the mission. Alcohol seems to be the escape of choice. The drinking becomes so frequent that the duty performance deteriorates, including missing formation, DUIs, lack of motivation, and a negative attitude reflected through verbal comments and disrespect. It is this behavior that the Chain of Command addresses through corrective actions, Article 15's, and rehabilitative efforts pertaining to the alcohol issue. When these rehabilitative efforts fail, the servicemember is discharged from the military and left to her own resources to cope. Unfortunately, MST issues are never addressed if the servicemember never reports and keeps the incident to themselves. I find this is especially the case when the lines are unclear with regards to sexual trauma. This leads back to Senior-Subordinate relations.

Upon retirement from the Army, I continued the *In Her Boots* efforts by working with Veteran Service Officers (VSO) in and around Texas, assisting with Women Veteran issues. Although working with some female Veterans in the more populated areas, more assistance was requested from VSOs from the rural areas. The Women Veteran population is very dense in these areas, increasing their lack of solidarity and allowing them to exist in their misery where populated areas tend to have more organized Women Veteran groups as support systems in the civilian world.

One day I received a call from a young Woman Veteran, who we will call SPC Jody. Specialist Jody lived in a rural area about five hours from my location. After speaking with her, I identified that the first thing she needed to do was register in the VA system. You see, SPC Jody reach out to me through the *In Her Boots* program. She was broken, broke, homeless, scared, and responsible for two children. In her state of confusion, she did not know what to do. It was too much information for her brain and emotional state to process even with direction and guidance. She clearly could not find her voice and needed someone else to speak up for her.

There is something about finding your passion, your purpose; you will do anything to accomplish your mission. For me, the *In Her Boots* program is my passion, my purpose. To assist female servicemembers and Woman Veterans to be all they can be. Although our primary mission is prevention before reaction, we cannot ignore the damage that has already been inflicted.

I drove the five hours and met SPC Jody at her respective Vet Center. As we walked in together, we were greeted by a little old lady behind a worn desk. The place was nothing more than the proverbial hole in the wall. Everything in the area was antiquated. I asked the lady if we could speak to a counselor. She proceeded to inform us that the counselors were for the men who served in the military. So, I asked, "what about the women?" She said, "the women sit out here, while their husbands go in and speak to the counselors." The hair on the back of my neck flared up, and I went into full defense mode. I proceeded to say in a booming, authoritative voice, "ma'am, you are speaking to two combat war Veterans. I have two tours in Iraq, and she has two tours in Afghanistan; now I will ask again, can we speak to a counselor?!" About that time, the door flew open from one of the offices, and this old-school Vietnam Veteran walked out, asking if he could help me.

I introduced myself as Major Lisa Bass, retired Army from the *In Her Boots* program, and said, "this is former SPC Jody." He immediately invited us into his office. (I point out how I introduced myself because, when one states their rank in the military, it reflects the level of responsibility achieved. The reality is if SPC Jody had gone in alone, more than likely she would have left and never returned when confronted by the receptionist. If she did get past the receptionist, the level of urgency to address SPC Jody's case would not have been met. She would have fallen into a red-tape system with no immediate relief for her situation.) The counselor was very helpful in getting forms signed and processed immediately. However, when it came to the issue of MST, he was very uncomfortable. It was as if he did not know how to address the problem or even what questions to ask to dig deep enough to identify what help SPC Jody needed. The absence of understanding MST's impacts leaves a counselor only dealing with surface-level issues and not the core problem. Procedurally, questions addressing Woman Veterans are not addressed often in this office. The counselor provided me resources to contact in their area that helped to find housing and employment assistance. The fact I was able to be SPC Jody's voice for a moment in time gave her the needed strength to get back on her feet and seek the medical attention so desperately needed through the VA system and to file her claim.

Unfortunately, when working with woman Veterans, a pattern begins to develop. With a little extra help and guidance, I have found that they can pick themselves up and get their life back on track. The problem is they cannot sustain that new course on their own. Without them being directly accountable to someone, or seeking help to address the issue that landed them in the situation, they will invariably revert to their old destructive ways. Their pattern will begin again. Once the alcohol has become the coping mechanism for female servicemembers or woman Veterans to deal with their pain caused by MST, the alcohol abuse must be dealt with first before anyone can assist in the healing process. Functioning alcoholics can become master manipulators in their quest to hide their dependency. That was the case with SPC Jody. After addressing her immediate need for housing and receiving donations for furniture and other household necessities, we secured her employment and childcare. We worked together and tailored action items specifically for her with accountability measures to be achieved. She was enrolled in Alcoholics Anonymous (AA) and assigned a counselor.

Once SPC Jody became comfortable in her environment, she began to miss her meetings; instead, grabbing the next beer became her priority. My mom often used the truism, "Birds of a feather, flock together." The law of attraction states "like attracts like." Ye Chen states in her article, *The Law of Attraction-You Attract What You Are,* "all attractions are based on energy, vibration, chemistry, or whatever you may call it; it's all the same thing. You send out a frequency, and it attracts someone or a situation of the same frequency." As in the case of SPC Jody, she quickly met new people in her apartment complex who also liked to drink. They eventually became her support system. The drinking episodes became nightly in the parking lot. She began dating one of the guys in the group and ultimately lost her job because she was too hungover to make it to work. She then decided to let her new boyfriend move in to help pay the bills. Then she got pregnant. Alcohol consumed both their lives, and the drama began. He moved out while she was pregnant, with no employment, which caused her to lose her apartment. Now she is back on the streets and in the same situation as when I first met her.

I was in constant contact with SPC Jody's AA counselor who gave me a piece of wise advice. She explained that alcoholics will take everything you provide them with no adjustment to their behavior. Unless the alcoholic decides on their own to get sober, they will move on to the next person who is willing to help them if you cut them off. They know how to manipulate and use people just to get to their next drink of choice. As SPC Jody was going through her decision-making process, I explained to her it appeared that we were riding the Mindbender rollercoaster at Six Flags. You see, this rollercoaster has its ups and downs, but then it has these two loops, and once it takes you on the loops, it puts you back where you were in the beginning. The fact is that you can only help someone so much unless they decide and are willing to help themselves; it doesn't matter what someone else does. I explained to SPC Jody that I would only ride the roller coaster's first loop with her. I would present the impacts of the decisions she was making, but if she kept riding the Mindbender, I had to get off and no longer ride it with her. That is what happened.

After a year of investment into helping a sister-in-arms, I had to walk away for my peace of mind. Until she was willing to get help for alcoholism, there was nothing I could do for her. She attended the Alcohol Substance Abuse Program (ASAP) while still on active duty. A check-the-block effort by the Command, as she attended ASAP in November of 2011. She was discharged from active duty in December 2011. She was sexually assaulted by her Platoon Leader in February 2011, shortly before going on Rest and Recuperation (R&R) leave, where she received a DUI. The Command didn't know she had been sexually assaulted by a superior, and she was heavily drinking for nine months before any action was taken to address the situation. Coupled with her promiscuous behavior leading to an unplanned pregnancy while being a single Soldier, she demonstrated an underlying issue that needed identifying and management. You see, SPC Jody did not possess the maturity or experience to recognize what had happened to her, much less understand the legitimacy of reaching out for help.

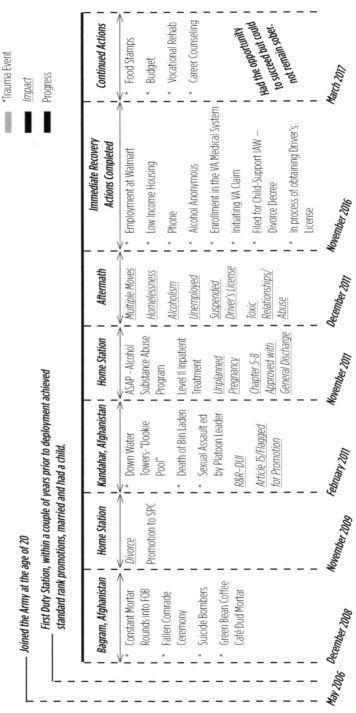

Legend
- *Trauma Event
- *Impact*
- Progress

	Bagram, Afghanistan	Home Station	Kandahar, Afghanistan	Home Station	Aftermath	Immediate Recovery Actions Completed	Continued Actions
	* Constant Mortar Rounds into FOB	*Divorce*	* Down Water Towers-"Dookie Pool"	ASAP – Alcohol Substance Abuse Program	*Multiple Moves*	* Employment at Walmart	* Food Stamps
	* Fallen Comrade Ceremony	Promotion to SPC	* Death of Bin Laden	Level II Inpatient Treatment	*Homelessness*	* Low Income Housing	* Budget
	* Suicide Bombers		* Sexual Assault ed by Platoon Leader	*Unplanned Pregnancy*	*Alcoholism*	* Phone	* Vocational Rehab
	Green Bean Coffee Café Dud Mortar		*R&R–DUI*	*Chapter 5-8 Approved with General Discharge*	*Unemployed*	* Alcohol Anonymous	* Career Counseling
			Article 15/Flagged for Promotion		*Suspended Driver's License*	* Enrollment in the VA Medical System	
					Toxic Relationships/ Abuse	* Initiating VA Claim	**Had the opportunity to succeed but could not remain sober.**
						* Filed for Child-Support IAW – Divorce Decree	
						* In process of obtaining Driver's License	
	December 2008	November 2009	February 2011	November 2011	December 2011	November 2016	March 2017

— Joined the Army at the age of 20

First Duty Station, within a couple of years prior to deployment achieved standard rank promotions, married and had a child.

May 2006

— 46 —

What was missed? The pattern. Unfortunately, her situation is not an uncommon one. First, SPC Jody was in the most vulnerable age group of 18-24. Not only becoming an MST victim, but at that age, the resiliency needed had not fully developed to process all the events that were taking place in her life and on the battlefield. Deployed for a year, leaving behind a husband and a baby, was stressful, resulting in a divorce, only to be deployed again a couple of years later, to encounter more incidents on the battlefield. Her nonchalant attitude, coupled with being divorced, signaled a more experienced or relaxed perception about relationships than most single women her age possess, making her prey to her predator Platoon Leader. During their deployment, he would always initiate conversations that did not involve anything about the mission at hand. He would go to her office looking specifically for her. She remembers the other junior ranking females saying, "girl, you know he likes you" as if she had a badge of honor for a leader to be attracted to her, a lower-ranking female.

Ironically, the junior enlisted know when something is going on. However, leadership misses it. Leaders are focused on the mission; they do not think twice about fraternization because it is forbidden under military regulation. They expect that everyone wearing the uniform abides by the same standard. More times than not, when a leader begins mingling with the junior enlisted, it becomes a game of secrecy. From the junior enlisted perspective, if the leader is the one crossing the line, regardless of the policy, it must be ok. They know there is a regulation, but when applied in their own lives it seems irrelevant, "their relationship" is so special, it flies above the rule. A classic, "familiarly breeds contempt" problem. The senior allows the subordinate to become close with their secret conversations, so that the junior enlisted now feels like she is an equal in the relationship, and knows enough about the military standards to keep it hidden in front of the Chain of Command. That is when the senior has the subordinate groomed to take advantage, knowing the subordinate will not tell. The predator is creating the scenario of an encounter that goes too far but denying it was sexual assault because the senior and subordinate were in a secret relationship.

The Platoon Leader set the trap. He finally groomed her into bed one evening. The next day, he treated her just like any other troop in formation, never speaking to her again about anything except things regarding missions. Her friends quickly noticed the difference and chalked him up to being another "dog." She agreed with them as the immediate perception was one of a failed relationship. What she felt down deep in her soul is abandonment, rejection, and betrayal. Her leader took advantage of her vulnerabilities. That was apparent as, within a couple of weeks going on R&R, she began abusing alcohol and got a DUI. As with many female servicemembers who have suffered at the hands of a predator leader, the downward spiral began. The Command is challenged with addressing the Soldier's alcoholic behavior instead of identifying why a good Soldier changed. No one looked at the pattern to identify where and when the change took place.

Soldiers usually remember something being mentioned about the VA benefits when they were leaving active duty, but "life happens," and they are faced with meeting their daily needs. Their military service with benefits and entitlements are a distant past. In interviewing them, I heard the same stories of MST incidents on active duty and overlapping struggles searching for jobs and facing challenges to remain in a home as a Woman Veteran. I have concluded they are in the predicament of homelessness or potential homelessness because of their decision-making process. It results from getting stuck in one of the five functions of the healing stages of MST. I've met female Veterans in their late 50's and into their 60's that experienced MST that are confined to their own homes from paranoia; they got stuck in a stage. These women left active duty over 30 years ago, and although they receive medical care from the VA, their mind is set and they will most likely live out the rest of their lives right where they are unless they heal correctly. SPC Jody moved back to another state where she had a family to help her out. While writing this in 2020, I looked her up on Facebook to see how she is doing, only to see her postings were about waking up drunk with friends and needing a job. As for the Platoon Leader, if he remained on active duty, he is either a Senior Captain or a Major.

The previous generation of women servicemembers did not talk about this. In my generation of women servicemembers, serving in the 1990s, we finally began to speak about it openly. The current generation of women servicemembers continues to break more barriers with voices and positions held. One can see the progress being made with women in the military by the increasing numbers of women volunteering to serve, especially as more doors are opening for women to serve in combat specialties. As we make great strides, it is being overshadowed by the negativity associated with sexual trauma, homelessness and suicide rates, leaving the civilian population to question, "why do we let women serve in the military if this is what happens afterwards?" The current situation is a two-front war. The active-duty female servicemembers continue to "find their voice," speak up and hold people accountable for injustice, regardless of rank, and get the proper care for recovery while on active duty. In the meantime, Woman Veterans help and assist the previous generations of women who served, who could not find their voice. Woman Veterans push forward to organize programs and establishments within the Veteran Affairs to address their issues. At the same time, lobbyists and the media want to focus only on the negative statistics. Unfortunately, this must happen now to stop the abuse for future generations while aiding the past generations of women who served.

The 21st-century generation of women servicemembers who entered Iraq and Afghanistan filled many "first female" positions in the service that are continuing onto this generation of women servicemembers, meaning, every day, progress is being made somewhere. With all that progress made for women serving in the military, currently, we do not get the appropriate and complete help to recover after a trauma. We do what must be done, and we move out! Like a Soldier, the aftermath of not properly healing can be profound and eye-opening when we leave active duty. Any female wearing combat boots knows those boots are a testament to their intestinal fortitude, their physical and inner strength. It is a statement to the outside world that they are equipped to handle what comes at them. However, it sometimes serves to camouflage the pain they may be hiding inside. It can even fool them into believing that the boots represent, they are above the need for proper care, that they would be considered weak, not living up to the standard if they sought help to recover appropriately. They do not need any help; they believe they are just fine, when nothing could be further from the truth.

Twenty-two Veterans committing suicide a day is most alarming, especially as the percentage of military females increases. The homeless female Veteran rate has increased by 140% since 2006, with 70% suffering from PTSD because of MST.

Why? What message is being sent to women about joining the military, that when they raise their right hand to serve our great country, it is only a matter of time until one will lose her life, either through combat, suicide, or even being murdered by their brother-in-arms? Life is hard enough without this stigma regarding women joining the military. The Army has a motto of "Never leave a fallen Soldier behind." The reality is that underdeveloped or predatory leaders in the military are creating the conditions for a female Soldier to fall and be abandoned by the organization they chose to serve. Prevention is in the patterns. It's important not only identify your own patterns, but patterns of others. Identify if you are being groomed for a potential assault. Identify what underlining problem may exist, instead of just addressing surface level issues. Unfortunately, sexual assault and sexual harassment are systemic throughout our society. If we continue to bind together as a *Sisterhood Against Sexual Assault,* whether or not you are in the military, and continue to find our voice, we can hold accountable the predators among us.

THE PREDATOR

Clarence Wilson, Sergeant Major (R), Chemical, Army

*Knowing is half the battle, the other
half is applying that knowledge.*

-Unknown

IDENTIFYING PREDATORS

There is no "creature from the black lagoon" that is easily identifiable as a predator. They could be brothers, step-brothers, fathers, step-fathers, godfathers, godsons, husbands, grandfathers, grandsons, uncles, nephews, significant others, and friends that we know and love. A predator fits the mold of every male figure in your life.

He can also be a serviceman, and he is a male with an attraction for the female species. Being in the presence of women makes many (and perhaps most) men act strange, so you have to use discernment for every situation because not all men are dangerous. The effects of women can be like kryptonite to Superman. In other words, you are more powerful than you know!

The predators that attack our women in uniform are sick. Somewhere along the way, something went wrong. There was a point in time where the mental capacity of this individual got off track. Professionals have tried to pinpoint characteristics in a sexual predator to develop a profile, but most of this information is collected after the fact, and the truth is, anyone could potentially be "that guy." Vigilance is the best form of defense. Awareness of people, places, and things will help you to recognize a potentially dangerous situation.

Predators seek to steal and destroy everything that you are and believe in. He comes to take you to the depths of hell and back. I believe that most don't desire to kill because they gain satisfaction from knowing that every time you think about what happened, he is violating you over and over again. We, as human beings, are creatures of habit. We have a routine that we follow on a daily basis. It is true that we have variations in our schedules and the unpredictable, but we have a schematic that we follow. A predator is likely to exhibit the same type of pattern. He is calculating and perverse. He stalks his prey and patiently awaits the opportunity to strip you. This coward seeks to minimize you, make you feel ashamed and alone. Predators feel with their hands while normal people feel with their hearts. They don't care about you, your families, or the law. They are manipulative and can literally charm the pants off you. If what he is selling seems just too good to be true, it probably is. If his interest in you is for sex, and not your friends or your worth, this could also be a sign that you are in the presence of a predator.

Often there is no real way of identifying an assailant before he acts out. Servicewomen are duped by the likes of male friends in uniform, who form a relationship and bond with the victim over time. They do whatever's necessary to gain the upper hand. They will include you, pay for you, hang out with you, and even defend you. It's all trickery, and his motives are not what they appear. He will learn your patterns, likes, dislikes, and vulnerabilities. At some point, he may even seem possessive, but you will think that he is your protector, and it's sweet. As soon as he feels that he has accomplished what he set out to in your relationship, he will formulate his plan of attack. Don't be fooled by excessive acts of kindness.

Someone could be watching you, and you have no idea that he is. You may not even know that he's there, but he watches your every move. He is a stalker who is unassuming. He hangs out in the crowd.

He may even get close enough to touch his victim or speak to her. He is playing charades. No one knows what he is up to but him. He fits in with others and never appears out of place. He wants to know your habits. He is recording your mannerisms as you move about and participate in different activities with your friends. He has scheduled his life around yours and knows when you are most defenseless. He just might be arrogant enough to make eye contact shortly before he makes his move. When your guard is down, he will assault you.

Some predators appear very rational. He may be in a position of authority and leadership. He may be well respected by other servicemembers, peers, and leaders. He could be a brother or father figure to some unsuspecting young woman. He is the predator that is well versed in areas of coercion and deceit. This predator is filled with boldness, confidence, aggression, and takes pride in exceeding established standards. He is often called the ultimate leader and coach, but he has a past that no one is aware of. He has a history of abusive behavior against females that have never been exposed. The abuse may start as a minor touching as a sign of reassurance or appreciation. The gestures begin to increase with stimulating conversation. He may even give you something of significance to make you feel that you are different from the others. You may be receptive for a while, but he's just buttering the buns, basting the turkey. When the opportunity presents itself, he will move in with aggression and take what he truly wants.

Predators walk around in the same environment as we do. They are staring us in the face every day. They are even members of our team. There have been complaints about how he looks at the female servicewoman, whether they are looking in his direction or not. He seems pretty naïve and almost to the point of sheer ignorance. He is the serviceman that is laughed at and sometimes lends a smile back at you. He is quite disturbed under that peculiar exterior, and leaders have a feeling that he could actually harm himself or others. But he has never been in trouble, disobeyed orders, or instructions. The obvious thing to do is to observe and communicate with this individual to get a sense of whether he might be capable of violence. Again, he becomes a serviceman who is passed by, viewed as insignificant, and the end results are sexual assault or even fatality. We just never know what will happen, but we can recognize warning signs, and it is better to assess the person or situation than to be sorry you did nothing.

Some predators are just mad, upset, and disgusted. It may not be directed at any single thing or person, but the behavioral patterns are disturbing. These are the characters that walk a thin line but never cross it. He has an opinion on everything and challenges every order. This is the serviceman that wants very badly to be a civilian but understands the consequences of a dishonorable discharge. He is a barracks lawyer who knows just how far to go before he's violated an article in the Manual of Courts-Martial. He is aggressive and vulgar when working with others and has no regard for anyone but himself.

When our comfortable lifestyles are disrupted, it makes us irritable and angry. As we look deeper at who our predators might be, we have to start looking first within our inner circles. Understand that everything is not always what it appears. Who are these people that you call friends? The saying "keep your friends close but keep your enemy closer" is not a cliché. Servicemembers form alliances and cliques just as in regular society. Servicemen and women come together to form these pacts for various reasons and develop a nearly unbreakable bond. When servicemembers feel that they have been dealt an injustice, they look for an outlet. Often, we find individuals coming together based on a commonality of disciplinary infraction or an unjust situation.

A predator could be the servicemember to the left, right, front, or back in a formation. He could be the leader of a particular organization. A predator could have a history filled with violence against him, himself, an offender, or both. Predators have been found with mental and social issues. Some have even been friends with their victims. The fact is that the violators of the Sexual Harassment and Assault Prevention policy will not divide the support that stands with a united front against them. Everyone that is knocked down, we will pick up, build up and encourage, proving their assailants wrong

Often times, female servicemembers are victimized over and over again through careless interview processes by immature, uninformed leaders, as well as systems that can be insensitive to the offense committed against them. As a result, many servicewomen do not report a sexual offense against them at all. In the *Annual Report on Sexual Assault in the Military,* the Department of Defense estimates that fewer than 15% of military sexual assault victims reported the matter to a military authority over the past six years. (pg. 53, 2012)

Every sexual assault case in an organization is seen as a black eye for the Command, and it causes a chain reaction of events that disrupts daily organizational activities. These organizational changes pale in comparison to a victim's dreadful life-altering experience. Her hurt is very real, and she should not have to live through the speculation of what she did wrong. A conscious decision was made by the attacker to commit the offense, and he alone is responsible. The magnitude of the sexual assault and harassment issues occurring in military service must not be ignored, swept away, or covered. They have to be met head-on. Every representative person or organization that has a responsibility to the care, rights, and confidentiality of the victim should be held accountable. Negligence or incompetence should be grounds for immediate removal and retribution.

We've heard that there has been an increase in reported sexual assault and harassment cases within the military services, but what if the reason we see this growth is only because the current generation of servicewomen is bold enough to report it? There may be generations of servicewomen, who for lack of awareness, didn't recognize what they experienced was sexual harassment or assault. The system may have limited their ability to effectively acknowledge and report these incidences. Service programs have come a long way in sexual harassment and assault education. Active education is only a portion of the need in the prevention process, but it plays an important role. Unfortunately, the battle to stop this abuse rages on.

We are all creatures of habit. We often go about our daily lives in a pattern with little awareness of the things that happen around us. Between cable television and Hollywood movies, we are exposed to unimaginable scenes. Sex and violence dominate every form of media these days. With the growing popularity of social networking, video communication, and cellular phones, it has become increasingly easy to communicate sexual fantasies and desires. Stalkers can now sit behind a computer screen or cellular phone and wreak havoc on victims. It doesn't stop there. I don't think it can be determined if Hollywood is imitating society or vice versa.

Pop culture has definitely played a role in the evolution of sex and violence around the world. Sadly, it does not help our ability to recognize the sadistic behaviors exemplified by predators. The truth of the matter is that we could care less about what's happening to someone else as long as it doesn't happen to us. The sexual predators who roam our formations are individuals just like you and me. I do not mean to suggest that we are all predators, but you can be sure of the fact that no one knows what anyone else is truly capable of. A significant emotional event that takes place in our lives may cause irrational behavior. Based on our past experiences and level of support, we recover and move past it, but some people resort to violence in order to relieve their pain. My point is that there will be a response in some form or fashion. We are uniquely made and very peculiar people who deal with challenges in many different ways.

KNOW YOURSELF

While it is important to know who the predator is, it is equally important to know who you are, and I'm going to help you discover that! I just read your mind. You're thinking, "who are you to tell me who I am?" I'm so glad you asked! I am a husband, father, brother, stepbrother, grandfather, godfather, grandson, uncle, and nephew who is wiser because of the influences of a wife, mother, sisters, and daughter in my life. I "see you" through their life experiences. I don't claim to know everything about you; I respect you too much. But, if I could contribute an ounce of hope into the heart of a servicewoman, I think I owe it to you to give it a try.

First of all, you are mothers, wives, sisters, stepsisters, aunts, nieces, godmothers, and goddaughters who are essential to the creation and nurturing of future generations. You decided to join the all-volunteer military service at a time when you are called upon to deploy and fight in conflicts just as your male counterparts. You are assigned duties in the Army, Marines, Air Force, Navy, and Coast Guards, and have earned your place in history. There is no need to transform yourselves into an image of a serviceman. You have exemplified more courage to join the military than it took for a cowardly predator to formulate a scheme to attack you. Walk in the path of female trailblazers who fought to earn women the right to wear the uniform with pride and prestige. So, it doesn't matter who speaks out against you with prejudice, "assume your positions."

Don't walk around looking and acting like a damsel in distress. Playing games of these sorts could be a detriment to your health and well-being. You may be a very sweet and innocent young lady, filled with humility, but you do not have to be frail and naive. You do not want to project an image of weakness and insecurity. The signals that you send may attract more than your fair share of suitors, but there could be a sexual predator within the group. Ladies, I hate to break it to you, but a man will tell you just about anything that they think could persuade you, just as you would them. Manipulation is a dangerous act played out between men and women. Some of you may think that your looks can get you anything you want, and you are probably right. It may also get you what you do not want.

Encourage yourself and stop looking at someone or something to encourage you. Be very selective about the men that you allow to be part of your lives. Servicemen and women share a special bond that comes with the duties and responsibilities of sacrifice for our country, but we have a choice in personal relationships. Nothing is more damaging to your self-respect than being violated by a man that you gave your trust. Trust is earned, not given away. Many of you give your heart and soul to the very one seeking the opportunity to leave you physically and emotionally disabled. The military has a decision-making process to arrive at the best course of action (COA). Before you become a victim, you have to determine the best course of action. Changing the current, high rate of sexual abuse will require each of you to take responsibility for yourselves and uniting with your sisters-in-arms in a cause that is as big as the fight of women for equal rights. You can do it; you are more than survivors!

If you have never taken the time to get to know yourself, stop what you are doing and begin the evaluation. You can only be of help to others if you have come to grips with who you are, where you come from, where you're going, and understand that there will continue to be obstacles in the path of your destination. Learn to love yourself, or you'll never truly understand how to love anyone or anything else. You should also come to terms with what has happened in your past; accept it because you can't change it. I think it's important to remember what you've gone through. I know that many of you have been broken due in part to failures, abuse, neglect, or loss at the hands of a man. Those that haven't experience this personally have been close enough to see firsthand the aftermath. Forgive yourself for your transgressions and others who have wronged you. Be encouraged to learn from your past. Your objective is to replicate good, quality, life-changing experiences, and denounce situations of suffering. Trials enter your lives to build strength and character; don't let your past determine your future. Develop a zeal for life and living, as well as a humanitarian disposition. Take charge of your own life without reservation. You are protecting your virtue with wisdom and knowledge. Are you your sister's keeper? Perhaps you are.

Stand up for yourself with integrity and respect. Give yourself a fighter's chance to make it in any circumstance. Condition yourself for the environment that you have entered. You worked tirelessly to survive training and become a servicewoman when others, unfortunately, did not. Some of you still paid the price of abuse by trainers, but you made it through. Readiness is next to Godliness. Just because you prepare for battle doesn't mean that you'll always face one, but how you prepare could determine the outcome. Mental toughness will take you where physicality is limited. Always observe and evaluate what's going on around you, as well as situations that you are confronted with daily. You can be assaulted at any time, day or night. Be cognizant of where you are and evaluate associated risks—exercise caution when in unfamiliar territory. The term "territory" implies physical location, structure, people, and environment.

Remember that alcohol is a game-changer; when you consume alcohol in the company of anyone, your risk-level increases. Many people transform into an alter-ego after becoming intoxicated. It has even been said that a drunken person shows their true personality. I do not know that to be true, but you know yourself. When you choose to consume alcohol, do it in moderation. Ladies, do not put yourselves in a predicament where you are the only female drinking with a group of males. The only exception is if you have a sibling brother present that will not leave your side. If you know that your behavior turns flirtatious when you drink, take along a person that will not drink to watch your back. You need someone who loves you enough to shut you down and remove you from a potentially bad situation.

If you are entering a room or automobile with a male when there is no one to witness, always observe and enter last. Immediately begin to assess your situation. It only takes a split second for an assault to take place. Someone could be waiting inside for you, or the guy that is escorting you could take you down from behind. Always carry keys in your hands in this situation. Clinch your fist with the point of a key or other sharp object facing outward for protection. You should be the one to close the door without locking it. Even someone you are familiar with, who claims to love you, could assault you. Don't be fooled by the sweetness of his persona. He may be like a honey bee, producing and storing honey while awaiting an opportunity to sting you. The difference is that the pain will be greater than that of a bee, and the effects will last longer. You need to use proper judgment when getting into a car. Let someone responsible know where you are and with whom you're going. Communicate with someone by phone until you've reached your destination and then still periodically check-in.

We are very private people, and I know that you don't want others in your business, but in order to become less of a target, you have to think about your own safety. Whether on or off duty, you get dressed up, hair done, made up, and smelling good for many different reasons. One of those reasons may be to attract a male, but everything that looks good may not be good for you. Whatever your flavor: money, muscles, pretty faces, nice clothes, or ride, you will find it. Use restraint and discretion when deciding what to do next because he'll recognize your weakness. There is no need to play coy when you've exposed yourself. The wrong guy will exploit and humiliate you if given the opportunity. He'll start to take, take, take, and give less. Don't let looks, sex, or material things be the reason that you stay. If you make it that easy for him, it could likely elevate to abuse.

Avoid walking in poorly lit areas where someone might be waiting in the darkness for you. If you must, carry a flashlight in order to see your path more clearly. If at all possible, never travel this path alone. It's also a good idea to have a whistle to blow and startle an attacker. Use deliberate blows with your fists and elbows, head butts, biting, scratching, stomping, and kicking to fend off an attacker. Develop and build relationships with other female servicemembers who understand your struggles. Challenge and encourage one another to demand respect, be strong, proficient, confident, and knowledgeable. Accept each other for who you are as well as the unique qualities that you possess. Agree to stand together with dignity and respect and to always be a source of support. Become a society of servicewomen who care about what's happening in the lives of other servicewomen.

THE ROLE OF MILITARY LEADERS

Military leadership comes in a variety of styles and personalities. Many military leaders have no idea what type of leader they are or have been. Today's diverse and complex military has forced leadership upon many servicemembers that are ill-prepared for the degree of difficulty within the constructs of battlefield situations. Assessments could be a difference-maker in the development of valuable skills required by a military leader. The best thing that can be done for young leaders is to assess their level of competence and abilities, provide constructive criticism, and hands-on mentoring. They are the future, and to ensure that the generations of leaders to follow are successful, we have to take a personal interest in their success. Military leadership is complex and diverse. To be the best at it, one must nurture the internal leadership development process so that our servicemembers are led by the best that our military branches have to offer.

These leaders must be the driving force of prevention. DOD has committed to pouring extensive resources into the *Sexual Harassment and Assault Prevention/ Response Program*. These actions are admirable, but until senior leadership takes a more hands-on approach to educating Soldiers across their formations, subordinate leaders will not engage the issue with any veracity. We all have to be committed to the zero-tolerance policy.

The male servicemember that uses offensive language and gestures toward females as a form of communication lacks proper social skills and is not representative of how a man behaves. The man who responds in support of his fellow servicewoman speaks to the regard of self and other Soldiers. Our men in uniform are a special breed. They are courageous Guardians of Freedom and Human Rights. We share a covenant to support and defend the Constitution of the United States against individuals who have made themselves enemy to our country. This enemy comes in the form of American citizens as well as those individuals born of a foreign land. Predators who don the service uniform suffocate the fighting spirit of our servicewomen and are also that enemy. The mere thought of such cowards in our ranks is disgraceful to everything that we stand for.

The men of our services understand and live by the reinforced values of loyalty, duty, respect, honor, integrity, selfless service, and personal courage. The Army identified these particular values as significant to the development of the spirit of the fighting Soldier. Our men are aware that it takes teamwork to accomplish the goals of the organization. Our servicewomen represent a major part of that union and play essential roles in mission accomplishment. Real servicemen stand side by side with their female comrades-in-arms, supporting them through any challenge before them. We, men of honor and integrity, which wear and wore the uniform, stand united in the charge to combat discrimination, mistreatment, and abuse of our women in uniform!

COOKIES IN THE COOKIE JAR

Lisa Bass, Major (R), Engineer, Army

Respect yourself and others will respect you.

-Confucius

Regardless if you are from the G.I. Generation, Silent Generation, Baby Boomers, Generation X, Generation Y, or Generation Z, some things remain the same throughout each of the social groups in time, which is *human nature*. There are general psychological characteristics, feelings, and behavioral traits shared by all humans. One of those constants is the instinct of sexual attraction that begins in puberty. Raging hormones, peer pressure, or low self-esteem can lead to choices that could negatively impact one's future. As we begin to mature and start seeking a partner in life, males and females have different approaches to that goal, further complicating this journey in life.

I have six granddaughters between the ages of 14-20. I am not ready to be a great grandmother in my youthful age. They hear the same consistent message from me, "it is your job to protect the cookies in the cookie jar!" They giggle and say, "Nana!" I always reply with, "Don't Play, I know those boys are trying to get your cookies!" On one of their visits, we went out to have our nails done. My granddaughters were commenting on how pretty my nails turned out. Laughing, together they said, "ooh Nana, you are going to have to protect those cookies in the cookie jar!" My immediate response, "no I don't! I'm married; Mr. Bass is entitled to those cookies!!!" They were caught off guard, but got the message.

I know what is going on in the world of granddaughters; I am not naive. The hormones are running wild; it is human nature. However, it is my job to reinforce what their parents are trying to convey to their daughters, which is that they should expect to be treated with dignity and respect. Boundaries must be established to accomplish this. The concept of "hit it and get it" one-night stands does not meet that criteria. Everyone should expect to be treated with dignity and respect. It is a perimeter that should never be crossed.

Boundaries are not made up of what you are willing to put up with; they are those things that you are not willing to condone at whatever cost. Boundaries are based on your values. How you value yourself clearly sends a message to others around you. If a person does not pick up on your energy that conveys your boundaries, and begins to cross the line, then in confidence, speak to the person to establish the boundary. For instance, I have a boundary of not tolerating God's name being used in vain in my presence. Now, you cannot see that I have that boundary. So when people are speaking and use God's name in vain, I let them finish their sentence; I may even wait until the conversation is over, depending on the rhythm and tone, but I will call them aside and in confidence, say, "do not use God's name in vain." I say it in such a manner, there is either no response or an apology. I do not ask "please" or make it a suggestion. It is my boundary; therefore, it is a fact. I have never had push back. They show respect for me and honor my request. People will push boundaries to see if you will respond. If you do not, you have given them permission to continue to move into your space. Developing the confidence and finding your voice sets the foundation for others to see that you value yourself.

Finding your voice is no easy task. It makes us vulnerable; creating the possibility of being attacked either physically or emotionally. Many of us avoid our vulnerabilities in fear of being judged, hurt, retaliated against, or other failed outcomes. It is a defense mechanism derived from being emotionally wounded somewhere in our past or fear of an imagined retribution. It gives meaning to the adage of *having our walls up*. From day one in basic training, while in the front leaning rest position, we are conditioned to not question. As we are going into muscle failure, the Drill Sergeants are screaming, "we will tell you the when, where, what, and how! We will not tell you the why, you don't need to know why!" They strip us of our boundaries. The military rank and Chain of Command structure has been established. The trust develops with the Drill Sergeants because in the end, we realize they were training us on how to stay alive. Stripping our boundaries is essential in our military culture for the good order and discipline to accomplish the mission on and off the battlefield.

The Drill Sergeants also instill in us the military values. Think about it, when we join the military, we come from all walks of life representing every aspect of our country - cultures, religions, and values (or lack of them). By military design, we are all then taught the same set of values creating a standard to live by. In the Army, our values are represented in an acronym: LDRSHIP which stands for Loyalty, Duty, Respect, Selfless Service, Honor, Integrity, and Personal Courage. For me, these values were easy to accept as it lined up with who I already was. So, drinking that Kool-Aid was easy. These are values I still carry to this day, as they have never failed me. Have I struggled in some areas? Yes! We are growing, learning, and developing every day. I would say that Personal Courage was the one value the Army developed most in me. It seems my whole career, I was put in situations that this area was tested. Did I always succeed? No. But here is the thing; I do not believe in failure, only lessons learned. I understood that to grow, I have to stretch myself. I had to meet those uncomfortable situations head on. I lived enough life to know, if I do not just go ahead and face the situation I am in at the moment, it will circle back around. It is one of those lessons I had to learn in life to be successful.

It is hard to find our voice in a situation when we have so much at stake which creates our vulnerability. For me, I was very vulnerable as a junior enlisted Soldier. I was a single parent with children at my first duty station. Working in TDS (Trial Defense Service) in JAG (Judge Advocate

General), I knew I could have potentially been a fraudulent enlistment. Every day, I woke up thinking, "is this the day they find out that I was a fraudulent enlistment, and I am kicked out of the Army?" After all the drama in my life, I had finally found a place where I fit. I loved being a Soldier. I truly believe the fact that the post was deactivating was my saving grace as there were no deployments or field exercises to bring light on my situation. The mission for the post was to turn in all the equipment and close out hand receipts.

The SJA (Staff Judge Advocate), a female Major, was the hand receipt holder for all the property within JAG. The Chief Warrant Officer who managed the record keeping had received his PCS (Permanent Change of Station) orders to depart. At the rank of Specialist (E4), I was tasked to learn and assume responsibility for the record keeping and inventory accountability upon Chief's departure. What I learned became very beneficial when I took over my Command in later years. As the drawdown continued, the SJA's hand receipt was to be transferred over to one of the civilians. I would walk the guy around, accounting for each piece of property he was to sign for. On the surface, he was confident about his duty. However, when the time came to sit and go through the books before signing the documents and completing the transfer, he became squeamish. Not once but on several occasions, this man would literally move around in his chair like he could not get comfortable, then he would get up, pace the floor and talk to himself. Then he would say we would have to sign the documents another time and leave. There was a suspense on when this transfer needed to take place. It was my responsibility to ensure the SJA met her suspense. Chief had already PCS'd. All the Non-Commissioned Officers (NCOs) worked for the Criminal Law Division, which was separate from TDS. There was no one I could ask advice from regarding what appeared to be an abnormal situation. Someone above my pay scale assigned this guy the duty of becoming the hand receipt holder. Who was I to question that? But I had a duty and there was a suspense attached to it.

This is where those Army Values came into play as my guiding light. The conflict in the situation was because of those Army Values I used as my standard. Loyalty, Duty, Respect, Selfless Service, Honor, and Integrity were what I was trying to uphold in completing my task of the hand receipts. However, because of the dilemma and conflict, I had to muster up my Personal Courage to go see the SJA and explain to her why the hand receipts had not been transferred. I was an E4 Junior Enlisted Soldier, she was a O4 Field Grade Officer. I had never spoken to a Field Grade Officer without the presence of some other ranking individual escorting me and then I just listened; I never spoke. I was scared. My vulnerabilities kicked into high gear. I mean, what if she thought I did not know my job or that I failed a mission that now impacts her? Then, because I could not accomplish the task, I would be deemed not good enough to be in the Army. Then they would find out I was a fraudulent enlistment, and I would be kicked out. Then how would I take care of my family? Talk about a long list of paranoia thoughts kicking in, all because this man did not hold the same values and would not complete his task.

Regardless of my vulnerabilities, I had a boundary. My boundary was protecting my career and the life I had, which allowed me to provide for my children. I made an appointment to see the SJA prior to the suspense date for the property to be transferred. She honored the request but wanted the guy to also meet with us. So, now I had to explain to her the situation in front of him. I must admit, I was so nervous, I know my voice was shaky and cracking. I thought my heart was going to explode. As I tried to find the right words to explain the dilemma, this guy was pacing the floor and denying everything that I was explaining. I stated my case and then I was dismissed. The following day I was called back into her office where she explained to me the guy was no longer going to be the hand receipt holder and another person would be assigned shortly. She either believed me or he refused to sign or a combination of both. All I know is that I was able to get all property transferred before the suspense date. The fact that I had a boundary gave me the strength and courage to address the situation. The outcome produced confidence within myself and faith in the values I held close. Although the situation may have looked grim, and my vulnerabilities came to the forefront, I faced it. The outcome was not what I expected. It was positive. That ordeal helped develop me in finding my voice that I would use throughout my career. Courage builds confidence.

By knowing your values, you can develop and establish boundaries. Never compromise on your boundaries, they are there to protect you. Each time your line has been crossed and produces a negative consequence; it grows your list of emotional vulnerabilities. Past pains and hurts create a self-protection mode resulting from fear. That fear begins to hinder us from developing in a positive way. Growth comes from allowing ourselves to become vulnerable; putting ourselves out there and being open to possibilities and opportunities. The fear of exposing our vulnerabilities that may produce pain, embarrassment, or a sense of rejection can be crippling. I would venture to say, addressing these types of fears takes more out of a person than going into combat. Knowing your values, having established boundaries, and allowing yourself to be open to new experiences will build character. Instead of being closed because of your emotional list of vulnerabilities, trust yourself because you know your value and have set your boundaries. Consistency is the key, like a battle drill. By executing the same set of principles, others will quickly identify how you will respond to a situation, not only establishing trust but warding off people who may mean you harm. Your consistent pattern automatically lets others know what they can and cannot get away with, in dealing with you. People will test your boundaries to reveal your true character. We are all vulnerable at different points of our life, so in the day by day developing process, encourage yourself with this formula as a reminder:

Values + Boundaries - Vulnerabilities = Character

In our youth, we believe that we are invulnerable, without accountability. This is the furthest thing from the truth. Newton's Third Law of Motion states that for every action, there is a reaction. This principle is executed daily in the military. As a Private, you may show up where you are told to be, without a second thought. However, leaders planned that mission and considered the second and third order consequences to that decision. You also do this. For example, if you drive a car to PT (physical training) formation and are running low on gas, naturally you question, "can I get to formation and make it to the gas station afterwards? How much time will that take before I need to make to the next formation or work? If I push the needle too far, I may run out of gas and be late for everything." So, you decide to fuel up the night before, alleviating any possibility of running out of gas and making it to your formations on time without stress. You would have been accountable if you had run out of gas, even if it meant you were standing on the side of the road, seeking out assistance. That would be a consequence to your action for not putting fuel in your vehicle.

I have a friend who owns a prestigious financial services business in the upscale part of Dallas, TX. We have plenty of discussions on business strategies and client behaviors. She has also served in the military and in the corporate industries prior to becoming a business owner. In one of our discussions, she explained that she has an operating principle, a boundary, that she does not meet with married male clients without their spouses. She sets the condition, ensuring that a male client does not have any preconceived notions about their professional relationship and financial portfolio. For her single male clients, she explains from the beginning that this is a professional relationship only. Why does she do this? Because in the past, she has been propositioned by both males and females. She is a beautiful woman, both in spirit and body. Therefore, she knows she must be heavily guarded. The reason she must be on alert is because the standard she is striving to live by is, unfortunately, not universal; other women have entertained inappropriate behaviors, making such solicitations more common. When we allow ourselves to be reduced in value, this becomes a problem for everyone. If we do not stand together as a sisterhood, we allow low standards to become the norm.

Men of respectable values and behavior also know their boundaries, and make their boundaries known. On one of my deployments, myself and another male Soldier, who was the same rank, were tasked to work on an important project. It seemed like every waking moment and all our conversations were focused on developing this upcoming operation. Walking to work, walking home from work, walking back and forth to the chow hall, we were always talking about this project, ensuring we were not missing anything. Then one day, as we were wrapping up all the details, he asked if he could speak to me outside. Unaware of what was about to be discussed with me, I said, "sure." We went outside away from the other Soldiers, and he began talking. He continuously looked outwards; he could not look at me directly, which made me uncomfortable. During the time he was talking, he mentioned his wife and that he did not think it would be appropriate if we walked or sat at the chow hall together during meals. I was flabbergasted! What was he thinking? That there was something more than me focused on the mission? I mean, I have male friends that have been my friends for decades and never had an issue. I honored his wishes; yes, that meant me going to eat later or sitting alone in the chow hall sometimes. But that was ok; I personally had done nothing wrong. I was a female in uniform; I had not done anything to lead this man into thinking there is anything more to our relationship but the mission. However, me being me, still had an impact. I respected him more as he made known his values and established a boundary, even though it was his issue, not mine. Initially, I was upset, wondering why I could not be accepted as just another Soldier. The fact remained; this was a year-long deployment and regardless of anyone's boundaries, human nature will try to take over.

Women who have deployed know the concept of being "queen for a year." Some will use it to their advantage, seeking attention or even promotions that eventually tarnish their reputation. The negative consequences of our sister's actions harm the other females serving, as a lot of male servicemembers begin to expect female servicemembers of their rank or below to condone inappropriate behaviors.

For my granddaughters, their minds are not developed enough to truly understand these concepts; they are beginning to mature. It is why I continuously repeat that it is their job to protect the cookies in the cookie jar. So, if they find themselves in a situation while they are starting to date and everyone's hormones are on high alert, they already have a boundary identified. Rest assured; they are going to hear their Nana's voice in their head reminding them about those cookies. If they choose to let someone cross their line, there will be an unforeseen consequence. Advanced in my years, I do not want them to experience unhealthy pain creating a vulnerability that can potentially impact the rest of their life.

The mixed messaging that women send, either consciously or unconscientiously, determines the level of dignity and respect we receive. It is our responsibility to identify and understand what messages we are sending. Branding is one of the most important elements of business. A business brand makes a memorable impression on the consumers. It allows the customers to know what to expect from that company, establishes an identity that sets itself apart from their competition and sparks a connection with its audience. We each have our own personal brand. Bottom line, if you are advertising, they are buying. What we wear sends a message. When I was about 25 years old, I already had three kids, but you could not tell by looking at me. I had long flowing blonde hair, a beautiful southern golden tan and was built like a brick house; you know "36-24-36," and had nice, well-defined, muscular legs. No one could tell me anything!

One Friday night, my best friend and I, along with our husbands, were going out for a night on the town. Confident in my appearance, I wore a short black leather miniskirt with a tight-fitting low-cut top and a pair of high heels to match my outfit. After too much to drink, my husband and I got into an argument and I stormed out of the bar. I walked to the nearest gas station and went in to use the pay phone, as this was before we had cell phones. I called my girlfriend at the bar for her to meet me at the gas station, then went outside and waited. I noticed a police car kept circling around the building. I went back into the store, purchased a coke and asked the cashier why the police were circling. He did not hesitate to answer my question, "because they think you are a prostitute." It was as if I quickly sobered up; I was horrified by the thought of me, a wife and a mother of three, looking like a prostitute! I had dressed up sexy for my husband. However, others did not know that and formed their own opinions of me. Luckily, I was not arrested for the suspicion of prostitution. It's scary to think of the consequences that would have had on my life. I learned early that some attire is to be worn behind closed doors.

What does your brand say about you? Personal branding is not a new concept with the ability to post your life's story on social media. You know that you are deliberately creating what you want others to think about you. You may even have the attitude like I did, that I was confident in what my body looked like and was proud of it. But think about it, what are you really saying to the world, that your confident, beautiful, or independent and proud? What messages are others receiving? Does your messaging line up with your values and boundaries? Dignity and respect are talked about throughout our military career, that we are to give it and to expect it. I believe every human has an innate desire to be treated with dignity and respect, regardless if they have an attitude, are rebellious or are humble and kind. Does your messaging state that you want to be treated with dignity and respect?

In attendance at a Veterans' business conference, I sat with 11 young high-speed male Veteran entrepreneurs. One of them asked if I knew about some Instagram pages and what active duty military women were positing? I said "no," so he pulled up the page and proceeded to show me. The postings consisted of females in uniform on one side of a picture and the other side was the same female with a thong bikini, some with even less on. All the guys admitted they followed those pages, and one said, "I look at that when I am on the toilet." They all laughed in agreement, verifying they do the same. I ask you, is that Dignity and Respect? What personal brand is being conveyed?

We do not know what the future holds or what opportunities may come our way a decade from now. Pictures speak a thousand words. Supreme Court Judge Kavanaugh had to defend his character and adult reputation against his youthful ventures that were documented in a yearbook during his confirmation hearings. Can you imagine how easy it is now days to research someone's past? More and more, employers use social media to investigate a potential employee. Before social media, one would go to an interview and the employer would hire them at face value, then watch to test if what they said in the interview process matches up with their production. Now, they can interview and then check the applicant's profile on social media to verify if what they said is who they are portraying, then decide if that is the applicant they want representing their company.

Who knows if the leadership in the military uses social media profiles to determine if someone is ready for a promotion to lead? During a Fox Sunday football interview, Patrick Peterson from the Arizona Cardinals delivered a message for young leaders that describes the process of leadership. He stated, "before you become a leader, success is about personal growth, and after success, it is about the growth of others." I must ask for the ones who think that their personal rights of freedom of speech are being invaded. If you are promoted into leadership, and you have social media postings portraying confidence in your body and that you are proud of your sexiness, what do you think your male subordinates' impression of you really is? It is naïve to think if these postings exist, that subordinates have not researched them. Sexy does not convey leadership. Anyone who matures during their personal growth and moves up the ranks wants their decisions and leadership to be honored, trusted, and respected. True leadership is based on character.

Regardless of what generation you represent, understanding those defining human nature principles that do not change over time can set you up for success in life. We are growing, developing, and maturing every day. Your values and boundaries are core issues that are already present. This is about taking the time to get know yourself, identifying your values and then *Finding Your Voice* to stand by them. Once you truly know yourself, that is when you are confidently ready to lead.

FINDING YOUR VOICE

Janice Lembke Dombi, Colonel (R), Engineer, Army

Differences can be a strength.

-Condoleezza Rice

Confidence is a fascinating concept. How do you quantify it? Are YOU confident? When I ask a room of servicemembers, "how many of you are confident?" About 98% of the people raise their hands. Then I arbitrarily select a single person from the group to stand up front to lead us singing the National Anthem. No one has sung yet. Here's the catch: confidence is situational. You may be confident in your job, a sport, or a specific skill. However, your confidence may not transfer over to confronting your supervisor or a peer about the topic of sex. The important thing to know is you can improve confidence in interpersonal and sexual relationships and *Find Your Voice.*

Finding your voice means you can speak up for yourself no matter how difficult the situation. You can speak up and demand to be treated with dignity and respect. You can speak up and say you are not interested in having sex. With more experience and understanding of how the military system works, confidence usually improves. Women in the military are confident, and I would be hard-pressed to find a woman that will admit she is not. Think about it. You left your family and friends and traveled across the country to a base or college where you didn't know many, if any, people. Your military training cadre made sure you learned your fundamental skills to march, fire weapons, and throw hand grenades. Then you had service-specific skills training like arming missiles, repairing radars, and building bridges. The military made sure you received basic indoctrination in the military culture with customs, courtesies, and jargon. These first steps take a high level of confidence that many people outside the military just don't have. There is, unfortunately, a large gap in military training.

The military does not teach you how to *Find Your Voice* and avoid or defuse unhealthy interpersonal relationships or encounters. Everyone receives the same M1A1 training. The military teaches basic skill sets, they teach how to give respect to leadership, but not how to demand dignity and respect for ourselves. While confident in most situations, interpersonal relationships can be more challenging. Women want to fit into their military team so fiercely; they ignore anything that might suggest they are a woman and, therefore, different. To many women, the fear of being different or an outcast from the team is more frightening and a worse outcome than having unwanted sex. In prison, solitary confinement is the worst penalty for an infraction of rules. Many women believe if they are "one of the guys," it will avoid solitary confinement. I was the same way. Like many military women, I was proud to be "one of the guys." To me, that meant fitting into my team without anyone noticing I was different. I was a tomboy growing up, so this was just an extension of previous behavior. It wasn't until I was 28 years old that a peer told me they never thought I was one of the guys; I was one of the Officers and Engineers, but never one of the guys. Nothing changed in how they treated me, and I was still a valued member of the team, but this information helped me understand the onus was on me to control interaction as a woman, not just as a teammate. You will never develop confidence pretending to be something you are not. Be authentic. It is not only OK; it is great to be a woman in the military. The institution belongs to the American people, not to men. Accept you will never be one of the guys and allow your confidence to soar.

Many women want so badly to be one of the guys; they allow people to treat them in degrading and unhealthy ways. Not wanting to make waves, many women just laugh along with the group or suffer in silence.

They don't recognize the behavior as sexual harassment. They don't identify the behavior as disrespectful. If confronted on the subject, many women say, "I don't mind." You should mind. If you cannot *Find Your Voice* and say something to stop the inappropriate behavior, get up and leave the group. This sends a message that you are confident enough to stick up for yourself, and predators should not approach you. If you are more comfortable talking to a group member separately and giving him your viewpoint, he may speak against the bad behavior. I had a peer who would always put his arm around my shoulder when he talked to me. It made me uncomfortable. Instead of finding my voice and telling him not to put his arm around me, I started listening to the little voice in my head, "does he put his arm around guy's shoulder too? Am I too sensitive?" I talked to a friend about this. The next time we were in a group and the guy put his arm around me, my friend said, "take your damn arm off of her!" It never happened again. Having a man as a second voice can help you, so the group doesn't just blow it off and say you are "just too sensitive." Of course, I should have told him myself, but I was on my confidence-development journey. Demanding respect is not about being sensitive. One-third of sexual assaults begin as sexual harassment. Set consistent conditions, so your superiors and peers know you are not afraid to make waves. Use your resources and protect yourself.

Understanding self-respect and the link to confidence is not an easy concept either. Everyone enters the military with a different background based on experiences, including childhood upbringing, previous sexual assaults, society expectations, culture, media images, friends, and work environment, to name a few. You are immersed in your world so profoundly you may not recognize the bigger picture and where your confidence level fits in. When involved, we may lose the critical eye to recognize what affect the activity has on long term self-respect and confidence. As an example, a junior Marine ran to the smoke break area beaming with excitement and joy. She proudly reported to her fellow Marine female friend that her entire squad groped her, and she "didn't even cry." Under no condition is this behavior by the men acceptable. Some of the men may have known the activity was not appropriate, but they submitted to the pressure to conform too. Other women report sitting quietly as their peers discuss pornographic photos of military women they shared on social media. This disrespectful treatment chips away at confidence, usually without your knowledge. When someone says or does something degrading, do not laugh and resign yourself to being "one of the guys" —after all, "boys will be boys." We expect more and need to demand more when men or women misbehave. No matter how much you mislead yourself that you are one of the guys, many of your acquaintances will want to or try to have sex with you. Fine-tune your antenna to recognize disrespectful behavior and confidence-chipping activity. Sometimes weakness in confidence is not apparent until tested under pressure. That is what happened to me.

I never wanted to be in the Army, at least not until the month I enlisted. I wasn't sure what I wanted to do after high school, but I never considered the military. I didn't think I could go to college either. With five kids in the family, I knew finances were tight. My family never talked about college. I didn't know anyone in college. I didn't think of it as a possibility, so there wasn't anything to research, evaluate, or plan.

I always studied hard in school, did all my homework, and earned decent grades. I played varsity basketball and softball; and also played trumpet in the school band. At 14, I took jobs picking apples at a local orchard, babysitting, and delivering newspapers after school. I volunteered one afternoon a week and on Saturdays to help with a recreation program for special needs adults and teens. I began working at a local Jack in the Box as soon as I turned sixteen. By seventeen, I was one of two shift leaders and, along with our manager, was the "adult" leadership at our award-winning fast-food restaurant.

I learned my work ethic from my parents. My mother was an executive secretary until my older brother was born. Then she stayed home to care for our family, including her ailing father, my older brother, twin younger sisters, and younger brother. My father frequently worked overtime at his job as a telephone installer. In the days before microwave ovens, his meal was often a plate warming on the stovetop, long after the rest of the family had finished dinner. One day, in my junior year of high school, as I left to catch the bus, my mother told me to study hard to go to college. Go to college! I wasn't sure what that meant for me, but I knew it was an exciting opportunity to go somewhere else and do something different. I didn't have a plan or know what I would study. After some thought, I just figured I would likely "do something in business." Based on my former experiences, I would undoubtedly define myself as confident.

I went against my father's desire that I should go to a local secretarial school and made the decision to leave New York State and go to a small liberal arts college in rural Virginia. As a freshman, I didn't get any of the subjects that I wanted and found myself in several math and science classes. I was silently lamenting my destiny of sitting in class all day when I saw an Army guy trying to get students to enroll in the brand-new Reserve Officers Training Corps Program (ROTC). Bottom line: I took an ROTC introductory leadership class so I could get out of the classroom. According to the Major, I would be able to canoe, rappel, hang glide, and experience other exciting activities, all without a military obligation. I especially enjoyed the ROTC classes that emphasized orienteering with maps, compasses, and running through the woods. We had lab one day a week, and would wear uniforms and march around a soccer field for a couple of hours. I never imagined marching around a soccer field would come in handy.

One day, an Army recruiter came to class and told us about a program where we could enlist in the Army Reserves, attend basic training one summer, return to college for the year, and attend individual training for a military skill the second summer. By the time we graduated from college, we would complete our military commitment. As I mentioned, I never wanted to be in the Army. I did, however, want to go to basic training to see how I would do. With this new split option program, I could go to basic training, have a summer job for two years, and not have to be in the Army! I enlisted and reported to Ft. Jackson, South Carolina, to begin as a member of a 50-woman platoon in a company with 200 men. The Army eliminated the Women's Army Corps months earlier and initiated co-ed basic training. My newly honed ROTC marching skills made me an asset to the unit; in fact, I looked like General Patton compared to the rest of the recruits. My Drill Sergeant appointed me squad leader the first day, and eight weeks later, I was on top of the world, earning recognition as the distinguished graduate of our 250-person company. I even gave a speech at the graduation ceremony.

At the end of basic training, I considered myself very confident. I remained at Ft. Jackson for a week after graduation to out-process for my return to college. Only a few women remained in our barracks, supervised by drill instructors consolidated from other platoons in the company. Late one afternoon, a Soldier came to my barracks to tell me I had duty that night. I was sure I did not and named the woman scheduled on the duty roster. The Soldier told me the woman did not have to pull duty with the Drill Sergeant that was on duty because she reported that he "fraternized" with her. In basic training, "fraternize" spanned the scale of everything from flirting to sexual intercourse, so I had no idea what happened.

I quickly changed to the correct uniform and reported for overnight duty. At some point during the night, the Charge-of-Quarters Drill Sergeant came out of his office and called for me. As I got up from my desk, he grabbed and picked me up, trying to kiss me while he carried me back to his office. I struggled and finally got away from him. When he came toward me again, I yelled at him to leave me alone. I was scared, but I was also angry. The Staff Sergeant returned to his office and closed the door. I kept my eyes on the door for the rest of the night.

I never reported the incident. My rationale was that the other woman reported him, and nothing happened. No one would believe me. Since nothing would come from it, I didn't want to risk the Army delaying my college return. I am glad that I found my voice and got away from this predator but regret to this day that I didn't go the extra step to report the incident. It wasn't until I thought about it weeks later that I concluded I should have reported him. Maybe, because at least two women reported the same Drill Sergeant for "fraternizing," he might receive punishment. Perhaps I could have stopped the Staff Sergeant from sexually assaulting the next Soldier who could not find her voice.

The military should have provided me with confidence-building training to address predators and reduce my learning curve. Clusters in the number of sexual assaults are the highest surrounding people in transition. This Drill Sergeant was a textbook predator, but I had learned to trust Drill Sergeants over the previous eight weeks. My antenna was down. A more mature woman knows to be aware of her surroundings and think like a gazelle. The predator will try to single you out, cull you from the herd, similar to how a lion goes after the isolated gazelle in the wild. Women pulling all-night duty were away from our herd. My regular trusted Drill Sergeants were no longer around as I transitioned from active duty to the reserve classification. Permanent-change-of-station, including arrivals at and departures from a duty station, and temporary duty (TDY), are similar transition situations with a high sexual assault rate of occurrence. The last days of basic training or advanced skills training are other common conditions where women may be more vulnerable to sexual assault. The women want to get out of the training environment as quickly as possible, and the predator sees this opening to get a woman away from her herd.

There are several other transitioning life events that separate women from their herd. The military should have taught me that life transitions are also openings for a predator. Going through a child custody battle or a divorce proceeding can also mark you as prey. The predator is looking for a woman out of her familiar environment. There could be a chink in her armor of confidence or a situation where she might not want to "make waves" by reporting a sexual assault. Learn to recognize when you are in a position where a predator is looking to cull you from the herd. Predators count on you being quiet. He is counting on you to accept anything to belong to the team...to be one of the guys. Surprise him. You are not a helpless gazelle. You are a confident lioness, calling the shots. Roar. Make a scene. He made a mistake targeting you, a woman with a voice. Finally, for your mental health, report the incident. If you are an assault survivor, get professional help to assist your recovery and to restore your confidence.

There are many pathways you can take to increase your confidence and find your voice. Education, leadership experience, and having a mentor are three of the easiest ways to decrease the learning curve. Don't confuse education with a degree. Education is much broader and possibly more important than a degree. A degree only reflects your knowledge in a series of classes. An education, with training, will help you to *Find Your Voice* under stress.

There is a tendency for servicemembers to decide to postpone life until they get out of the military. Don't do it. This "I'm going to wait till I get out" philosophy is restrictive and puts you in a weak position. When you say you are waiting until you leave the military, you are really telling yourself, "I can't" or "I'm not good enough." These are insidious words that prevent you from THRIVING. The wait-till-I-leave philosophy also puts your intellectual development and maturity on hold. It is like a time machine waiting to jump several years to the future where you discover life passed you by. I had officer friends, who, in their 30s, lived in a room that looked like a college dorm. They had stick-like Army furniture, a trunk for a coffee table (not as a decorating idea but because the table options were either the trunk or the laundry basket), not a book in sight, and sleeping in an Army issued twin size bed with an olive drab green wool blanket. The only item that personalized their space was a big television where many would spend every evening. I'm not commenting on their design style, but their attitude to "wait until they got out of the Army..." to get furniture, go to school, join a club, to live. They are putting life on hold instead of developing confidence through growth.

Of course, you have to follow your services regulations, but you still have tremendous flexibility, even with unpredictable work and deployment schedules. Get out of the barracks, dorm, apartment, ship, or officer's quarters. Don't postpone your life. You may not have many choices during duty hours. Still, I can assure you, your life will not improve in a bar or club, endlessly playing video games, or watching television until 2 a.m. These activities should be recreation and occasional. If this is a nearly daily occurrence, you are postponing your life.

My first Battalion Commander had a duty-plus-one policy that I self-imposed for the remainder of my career. He required everyone in the unit to volunteer at any outside-of-work activity that had people involved. We had to include the duty-plus-one on our evaluation support form. As a Junior Officer, I coached a youth basketball team for one year and was an assistant scout leader for another. This duty brought me into the community and gave me a chance to lead in an area not related to my rank or work position. I met several adults outside of my unit, so I wasn't surrounded by like-minded people all day. I had to *Find My Voice* in an area out of my work comfort zone. As a bonus, it also gave me a social outlet that didn't involve clubs and alcohol. When my Commander directed me to volunteer for community service, I remember I was initially mad because I resented having a requirement in my off-duty time. I didn't realize it at the time, but my Commander was reducing my learning curve. It didn't take much time to adjust, and soon, I enjoyed my plus-one activities.

If taking college classes doesn't interest you right now, I understand. Explore your interests that are not academic. Take courses at the base community center or adult education classes off base. Learn how to play an instrument, do woodworking, learn a language, join a softball league— you fill in the blank. Live each day like you are making the military a career. You will make better choices regarding your off-duty time and participate in activities that will develop your confidence. I was in the Army for ten years and still had not decided to make it a career. I told myself I would stay while I was still having fun. Your current job might not be ideal, but your after-work community involvement can make it fun/and or rewarding. As a bonus, you will develop confidence by making yourself more valuable, gaining skills, and adding to your accomplishments list. Remember, in the military, your next job and new boss are just around the corner.

No matter how hard you try, and no matter how far you progress in rank, there will always be something you cannot handle by yourself. You will need someone to help you get your voice heard. For this, I recommend finding a senior military person that you trust and in whom you can confide. It would be even better to find a woman servicemember as your mentor, but this may be difficult given the lower percentage of women in the military. My guidance is to Find Your Voice and ask a senior woman if it would be OK occasionally to ask her questions. Sometimes the word "mentor" scares people off because they anticipate a large time commitment and special training. Asking questions doesn't sound like a big imposition, so you can start a relationship. Someone outside your Chain of Command is preferable if you are having an issue with someone in your Chain of Command. The mentor might be less willing to assist you if the situation involves her Commander too. If you have a trusted person, you can go to her when you are over your head. I'll provide a couple of examples:

When I had been at my first post exactly one day, I was required to see the Brigade Commander (the most senior person in the organization) for my routine "Welcome to the Brigade" office call. I reported as directed, and my Commander told me to take a seat. The Colonel opened the conversation by telling me that I did not have any right to be an Engineer. He then told me I couldn't say he discriminates because his headquarters Company Commander was a woman. He concluded our talk by telling me not to "go screwing enlisted men." He said he wouldn't say that to a male unless he did something to warrant it, but I needed to be told. I was in shock. I definitely didn't find my voice. I was confused about my future in the unit if the senior ranking person didn't think I had the right to be there. Afterward, my boss, the Battalion Commander, asked how the meeting went, and I was embarrassed to tell him. Yes, I was embarrassed, but I did *Find My Voice*, and reported what was said in the meeting. My Battalion Commander reassured me that I belonged in the unit and told me I could report the Brigade Commander for the inappropriate conversation but discouraged me as it would probably not lead to anything. It was enough for me to know my boss understood what happened, and I was able to work at my assigned duties without concern.

Two months later, the same Brigade Commander I mentioned in the "Welcome" office call approached me at a formal military social event. He told me Colonel Brown "was after my body." I stood at the position of attention, in my dress uniform, for the longest 45 seconds of silence in my life. Where was my voice? Why hadn't I been taught how to respond to an inappropriate comment or innuendo? After I had squirmed enough, he continued..." what I mean is, he wants you to go to Post Headquarters to work in Protocol." Again embarrassed, I went back to my trusted senior leader and told him about the inappropriate word choice and a possible move from my Engineer duties to Post Headquarters. My Battalion Commander probably rolled his eyes, but he ensured I remained in my current job, where I needed to be, working with Soldiers.

A couple years later, a fellow Company Commander in my unit told me there were pornographic photos of me circulating. She said she would find them and take them to the Battalion Commander and ruin my career.

These rumors were beyond what I could handle, so I went to my trusted senior leader, who also happened to be my Battalion Commander. Again, I was embarrassed to discuss the topic, but I told him about the threat if he heard a rumor about pornographic photos of me. First, he asked if there might be photos. I assured him there weren't. He was disturbed that a fellow Company Commander would behave so poorly. He had a theory about her ulterior motive, to draw attention away from a series of recent bad events in her unit. To remove himself from the equation, he passed the issue up the Chain of Command and arranged a meeting at the Brigade Commander's office. (Not the same Commander from the Welcome office call, thankfully.) The other Company Commander didn't know why we were summoned to the higher headquarters. When I told her, she couldn't believe I told our boss about the threat. The Brigade Commander asked the other Company Commander several questions about seeing the photographs-she had not. The Brigade Commander asked why she wasn't doing everything in her power to get the photos to protect my reputation. She did not have an answer. So, her whole plan to make me look bad backfired. By getting my trusted senior leader involved when I was in over my head, I took her power to hurt me away. It was uncomfortable after that, and the post was not big enough for both of us. Fortunately, I moved on to my next duty station. No matter what your rank or experience, there will come a time where you need advice or assistance, and a senior person can help develop the confidence to find your voice and retain your power.

The defense against predators is significantly strengthened when the junior woman has a senior female mentor to turn to for assistance. The predators would then know they are not only taking on the junior, less experienced woman, but also her senior mentor. Senior mentor women can also assist junior members in developing confidence to approach the Chain of Command to address a problem before it escalates into a sexual assault. This could significantly reduce the number of sexual assaults since approximately 1/3 of sexual assaults escalate from sexual harassment.

I talked to a young veteran who had been out of the military for about a year. According to her account, she liked the Army and would have stayed in longer, but her Company Commander said she must have sex with him if she wants to get promoted. I would love to have been her senior leader mentor. I would have her set an appointment to see the Commander on his open-door policy. I would then accompany her to the meeting and ask to hear about his promotion policy again. A senior mentor can give you advice and provide cover when a situation is beyond your voice alone. The predator is not just dealing with a junior or peer. He now knows a senior leader is aware of his transgression, a senior leader *With A Voice*!

A senior trusted advisor can also help you approach your Chain of Command. Here is one final example: ultimately, in the military, all activity returns to the Chain of Command to resolve. The sooner an issue passes this gate, the sooner you move toward resolution. A Soldier came to me because her supervisor said she had to change units after reporting that a Sergeant in the organization sexually harassed her. Sergeant Smith was upset because she did not want to change units. We were in a combat zone, and she didn't know any of the new organization's people. I asked Sergeant Smith if she told her Commander that she didn't want to leave. She expressed that she was afraid to approach him. I recommended seeing him during the Commander's open-door policy time and to bring a friend to provide moral support. She took my advice, met with the Commander, and he reversed the decision for her move. When two other women in the unit saw that she did not have to relocate, they had the confidence to come forward and file sexual harassment reports against the same Sergeant. The three allegations lead to a formal investigation of improper conduct by the Sergeant. The three women were satisfied with the outcome. A senior trusted leader may provide advice and top cover to help you *Find Your Voice* and retain your power.

Confidence is situational. When you have a broad base that involves many activities and a wide variety of people, you value less what one peer thinks and much more what you believe. It is with this newfound confidence you can *Find Your Voice* in interpersonal and sexual relationships. Be aware of your surroundings. If you are in transition— antenna up. If you are drinking— antenna up. Don't be a gazelle. Be a lioness. Lionesses are fierce. They do all the hunting in the pride. If you do not consent to what is happening to you, say it. In a clear, loud voice. Yes, *Roar*! No one is a mind-reader. If the predator doesn't listen, make a scene as it is the last thing the predator expects. He thinks you will do anything and put up with anything to be one of the boys. We all know... we will never be one of the boys. We are women servicemembers with as much right to our chosen profession and defense of the nation as the men because this is America's Military.

Thirty-three years after I raised my right hand and enlisted in the Army, I reached my mandatory retirement. I left my beloved Army at the rank of Colonel with four Master of Arts degrees, and a list of assignments as an Engineer, that included being the first woman to command a Division in the US Army Corps of Engineers. I had jobs that I never dreamed of, including building schools and clinics in Central and South America, teaching military history at the US Military Academy, West Point, commanding an organization of US Military, Department of the Army Civilians and Korean Nationals as we planned and worked on a 10.5-billion-dollar relocation program in Korea, to name a few. The military will give you numerous jobs and opportunities. You will make the experiences. When I enlisted in the Army, my father, a Korean War era draftee, gave me one piece of advice. He told me, "don't volunteer for anything." In my opinion, he couldn't have given any worse advice. If you get rid of your television, you'll be amazed at how much time you have in the evenings. Do not put your life on hold until you get out of the military. First, excel at your job, then volunteer, go to the fitness center, learn to play the ukulele—just get involved. It is outside your room where you will build confidence to *Find Your Voice.*

RISING ABOVE

Tammy (McKenna) McClimans, Colonel (R), Chemical U.S. Army

Don't let where you came from or bad things that happen to you define who you become...unless it's to become a better person.

-Tammy McClimans

I was asked to speak at a TF SASA's "Finding Your Voice" event in Baghdad, Iraq, in 2010 while on a one-year tour. I was a Colonel in the Army, and by then, I had about 32 years of active duty. I was hesitant at first because it would be the first time I had ever publicly spoken about being a rape victim in the military. Secondly, I avoided public speaking where possible because I have to take medication to reduce anxiety an hour before I speak. But I thought: *if not now, when?* Wasn't it time to share with other women/men about being a rape victim and letting them know it did not define the woman/Soldier/person I became? Didn't I need to tell them that this act of violence did not ruin me; that it did not define me, and that I should let others know it does not have to define them? So, I did. I was plenty nervous...but I am glad I did...and here's part of my story...

I was the oldest of five children. After the sixth, my mom was divorced. My oldest sister died at birth and was the reason for my mom and dad getting married. My younger sister died in an automobile accident when she was 17 while I was stationed in Germany, and my brother died two years later from a car accident after being in a coma for several months, also while I was in Germany. I can tell you; I was not happy with God back then.

We were poor and raised in Ohio. My mom supported us at first as a waitress at a little coffee shop in our tiny hometown. She went on to be a go-go dancer, and then a bartender after a knee injury caused her to give up dancing. Now she is a bar mom who sews and sells costumes to strippers. God bless her; she only had an 11th-grade education, but she always worked, and she is now 74 years old.

We lived in subsidized housing, took our clothes to the laundromat a quarter of a mile away in a shopping cart, and had our electric turned off on more than one occasion because we couldn't pay the bills. Still, my mom would take us all to see a Disney movie at the theater or see the Nutcracker or to Ponderosa Steak House now and then, when she'd make good tips. She made most of our clothes. We got by. I cannot say I always liked my mom, nor agreed with her parenting. She beat the hell out of us with belts, paddles, and switches while she held on to us by the hair, or made us hold each other down so she could beat the other one...we were too scared to turn her in for child abuse because we thought after they left, she'd beat the hell out of us again! I must admit, I was a bit rebellious growing up, albeit in a subtle way, more defiant than anything. I got put in a children's' home after I moved to my dad's house. My gram and pap adopted me in the last two years of high school. It was the best thing that ever happened to me. I did not want to disappoint them; I loved them so much, and they were my world.

So then came graduation. I did not have a clue what I was going to do, so I joined the Army because they offered me a great job as a counselor. I joined straight out of high school as a Private and went off to basic training. I was in the last class of the Women's Army Corps (WAC) and its associated Advanced Individual Training (AIT). My first duty station was out in the middle of no-where...and that is where I was raped by one of the Sergeants in my company.

It was a surreal experience. I didn't know the guy, but he was in my company and worked at the troop medical clinic. He saw me in the hall one day on the weekend and told me he had run across what appeared to be a prom picture of me and my prom date. He described the picture, and I knew which one he was talking about. He said he was going to go back by the clinic and did I want to tag along and grab the picture? I said "sure." In the late 70s, there were no discussions about sexual harassment, sexual assault, and rape, nor was there such a thing as a "battle buddy." Sure, I didn't know this guy, but why would I think something terrible would happen if I just went up to the troop medical clinic to pick up the prom picture he described? I was and still am a trusting person. My thoughts rarely turn negative, unless someone's behavior or words cause me to feel uneasy...and I never got those negative vibes from him when he asked if I wanted to go with him. I had no other plans that day, and it was just a short walk to the clinic...so I said, "sure...of course!" In hindsight and with much-needed awareness of predators out there amongst us, I would have asked him to bring it to me or have my girlfriend go with me...coulda, woulda, shoulda! I didn't. I was so young and trusting.

When we got to the clinic, he went to the records, pulled out my picture and gave it to me. He then asked if I wanted to see the rest of the clinic. I said, "sure." No one was there because it was closed, and it was the weekend. He showed me the x-ray room and asked if I wanted to get high. I said "sure" ...this was back in the early 80s before the Army started drug testing. I was just 19 young and did not want to feel like a (I struggle for the word), like a prude? Like I was not cool? I do not know, so I said "yes," and we smoked a joint. Then I started to feel uncomfortable around him.

I was not sure if it was the pot or what, but I said, "well, I better get back" or something to that effect. I did not want to say that he was making me uncomfortable because I didn't want to offend him if I imagined he had evil intentions when he did not. I got up to go, and he told me I was not leaving yet. There ended up being a struggle, and I started to scream even though no one would have heard me in that x-ray room with the door closed. He told me if I didn't shut up, he'd break my jaw. I tried telling him I was pregnant, but he continued to rape me. All I could think was how he could kill and drop me in a dumpster, and no one would be the wiser. It was awful. When he was done, we walked back, and he told me I needed to start getting him some money. I did not know what the hell he was talking about...I was scared, and it was as if I was walking in another dimension, as if it was all a bad dream. What the hell? The dude was obviously whacked. I was scared, humiliated, embarrassed, and numb, very numb.

When I got back to the barracks, I went to my dorm room and crawled in my bunk. I was shocked. Eventually, my best friend there, a PFC herself, asked me what was wrong, so I told her. She said we needed to report this to someone. I said, "ok;" it was like I was in a dream world. She went with me to the Military Police (MP), who took my statement. The MPs then took me to be examined by the doctors. After that, I had to see my Commander and explain again what happened. When I told my family, my dad wanted to come out and kill the guy, but I warned him that would only result in him going to jail, and we needed to let the court system deal with it.

Initially, I had to stand in every formation with my rapist because, of course, "you're innocent until proven guilty." Eventually, they transferred me to another unit until the Courts-Martial trial was over. He was charged with rape and sentenced to 10 years in prison and a dishonorable discharge, reduced to Private with loss of all pay and benefits.

I was nervous having to get up and testify because he just sat there staring me down with this hostile look on his face. Can you imagine how scared I was? I felt like I was the one on trial as they brought up what type of clothes I was wearing, how I dressed, and how many boys I had had sex with within my life—like that had anything to do with this guy raping me! But justice prevailed and he was sent to Leavenworth, and my girlfriend and I were both transferred to another duty station for compassionate reasons, because threats were made against our lives.

After that, I put it behind me and eventually met a guy at my next duty station who I married....but not two years later, I was informed that there was an appeal made alleging that there was some technicality in the instructions to the jury. There were two choices a) they would have to retry him like it was the first time he was tried and recall all persons that testified in the original trial to re-testify, or b) they could wipe his slate clean like he was never convicted and give him back all his pay and benefits and rank.

They asked me what I wanted to do. I said, "retry him." I was not looking forward to seeing him again or going back through the whole trial again and reliving those horrible memories, but he was guilty, and there was no way he deserved to get back all his benefits like he didn't do anything wrong.

Well, we went back, and he was retried and found guilty again. Since he had served two years, the judge said he was not going to send him back to prison because he would be released in a little over two years for good behavior. He did give him the dishonorable discharge, reduction in rank, and loss of pay and benefits. I changed my maiden name to my married name to prevent him from finding me after his final discharge. I put this event behind me...for the last time.

One of the things I learned from this experience is to trust my instincts, even if a person or persons gives me a hard time about not doing something/going somewhere. I am ok with not being "cool" or being labeled or whatever someone wants to call me because I will not do something or because I will not bow to peer pressure. I have learned the hard way that it is better to risk hurting someone's feeling because of a false impression than subjecting myself to a potentially harmful encounter.

I'm not one to dwell on anything for very long. Sure I ruminated on all the things I should have done, or could have done to avoid placing myself in a vulnerable position that a predator could take advantage of, but it happened. Thankfully life took hold and I was preparing for my compassionate reassignment. I didn't know where Ft Bragg was or what my job would be when I got there, where I would live, what opportunities I would find there...so many things to think about. I grabbed hold of those thoughts, let them consume me and blocked out any ruminations on his violation of my mind, body, and spirit. On occasion, if I found myself thinking about him or the rape, I'd change my thoughts to the next day, what the future unfolding before me could offer...eventually life and each day forward propelled me to the next. I grabbed hold of each day and dealt with it instead of dwelling on an event that was done, that I could not change. I wouldn't continue to let him victimize me further by allowing him to consume my thoughts.

I look back on my childhood and am glad it was not the best because I can appreciate how good life is now. I look back and smile at what was good and accept that my mom did the best she could. I do not have time to dwell on or carry around grudges...that is exhausting. So, I learned to cope through humor, laughing at myself and life, expecting that bad things may happen, that sometimes I will fail, but... in the end I am responsible for what defines me.

PASSION, PURPOSE, AND LEADERSHIP

Professor Jeff Willie, Senior Master Sergeant (1st Sgt), USAF Ret

The Law of Awareness states,
"You must Know Yourself to Grow Yourself."

-John Maxwell

Where did you come from? Where are you going? What is your plan to get there? Life isn't a sprint where a fire in your home awakens you, and you make a mad dash to save your life. Yes, at times, you may need to make a mad, emergency dash; but overall, life is a marathon with patterns of stops, rethinking, reflections, self-assessments, readjustments, and restarts. And by the way, the marathon is not over until the end of your life. After you make your end of life, final assessment, you will wonder "how was that marathon journey?" Did you fulfill your life purpose? Were you guided by your passion every day? How well did you lead yourself? Yes, our biggest challenge in life is leading *ourselves*!

Are we true to our passion and our purpose? My hope is that we all discover our purpose for being on this earth. Do we know our mission/calling? I believe we all have a unique mission in this life designed specifically for each of us. Your purpose is as unique as your fingerprint, different from any other person on the face of the earth. Yes, our hands are similar in shape but different in characteristics. Therefore, our purpose/mission may be similar, but unique in how we execute it. Mark Twain said it best, "the two most important days in your life are the day your born and the day you find out why."

"Why?" is the question we must continue to ask ourselves until we discover our WHY! And how do we discover our WHY, our passion, and purpose? During the majority of my 26 years in the United States Air Force, the law of attraction, and my heart's desires placed me in speaking and teaching opportunities. Therefore, to this day, I find myself drawn to speaking, teaching, training, facilitating, serving, and adding value to people; people are my business. The million-dollar question to ask yourself is: *how do I discover my passion and purpose?*

How many people do you know who are stuck in dead-end jobs or professions they despise? When you ask them why they are still working for company X or doing a particular job, answers may include (1) the pay is great, (2) I have limited skills, (3) I'm not qualified for other jobs, (4) my entire family has always been educators, lawyers, doctors, mechanics, etc. (5) I don't know what I want to do. I had the opportunity to mentor a Staff Judge Advocate (Army lawyer). A few minutes into our mentoring session, she admitted that she did not prefer to be an attorney. I asked her why she attended law school, took a state bar exam, and received a commission in the United States Army? Her answer did not surprise me. She stated her parents wanted her to become a lawyer. Her brother was an engineer. With the high expectations imposed on them by their socio-economic level, most in that culture worked in professions that did not align with their passion.

I asked what some of her hobbies were, her volunteer opportunities, and in what area of her life she finds the most joy. It didn't take her very long to answer the questions. She volunteers for a Boys and Girls Club during the weekend. Her passion and moments of joy were math tutoring, sharing life moments with teenage girls, and taking kids on field trips. The lawyer always wanted to be an educator. Fortunately, she is transitioning from the United States Army to become an elementary school teacher.

How do you reach your full potential...discover your passion? What delivers you the most joy? One of the first steps is self-awareness, and that may require an assessment to reveal blind spots to your true passion. Once you are aware of them, be willing to accept what they teach. To grow, you must know yourself and accept who you are before you can excel to the next level in your life. Awareness will reveal your strengths and weaknesses, your interests and opportunities. Awareness will help you set a course for where you want to go. And of course, every time you want to learn something, you must be able to take the new thing you've learned today and build upon what you learned yesterday to keep growing.

If you become aware of the steps you must take to grow toward your passion, doing what you want to do, you will begin to produce behaviors you desire and start attracting like-minded people. The Law of Magnetism in *The 21 Irrefutable Laws of Leadership* by John C. Maxwell says, "Who you are is who you attract." If you're growing, you attract others who are growing. This puts you in a position to begin building a community of like-minded people who can help one another succeed.

Stop, reflect, and ask yourself these questions:

- What am I doing, and do I enjoy what I'm doing?
- When I dream, what do I dream about doing?
- Am I surrounded or attracted to people that do what I want to do?
- Can I gain access to resources to do what I want to do?

As a man of faith, I truly believe if you have the right attitude, all things work together for your good. While I was active duty Air Force, before I became a First Sergeant, I was a Security Police, Security Police Instructor, and a Combat Security Police Instructor. When I entered the Air Force in 1977, I had no vision of becoming Security Police. The Air Force needed Security Police, and so that became my profession for 14.5 years. Because of my positive attitude, desire to serve others, my ability to communicate effectively, and desire to grow, I was surrounded by like-minded, growing, Non-commissioned and Commissioned Officers. After eight to nine months at my first duty station (Hahn Air

Base, Germany), I was selected as a primary trainer for Priority Security Area Entry Controller, responsible for training all newly assigned Entry Controllers. From assignment to assignment in the Security Police career field, I was elevated to key leadership positions. I executed teaching positions, evaluator positions, became an adjunct instructor for Airman Leadership School, keynote speaker for Professional Military School's commencements, and sought-after Master of Ceremony of key senior leadership retirement banquets. Again, you will produce behaviors that attract people to your passion when you are willing to grow. Carol Dweck, American Psychologist, states, "people with a growth mindset believe that their most basic abilities can be developed through dedication and hard work; brains and talent are just the starting point. This view can create a love for learning and a resilience that is essential for great accomplishment."

Now, allow me to offer a disclaimer to a small amount of success I achieved at this stage of my life. I have a story; you have a story; we have a story, and others need to hear our stories. My challenge to you is to share your story. Your story, your setbacks, and your triumphs could be the catalyst that moves the needle in someone's life closer to reaching their full potential.

Sharecropper parents raised me in the woods of East Texas. My father was born in 1910, the oldest child of eight children. His father, John Willie, died in 1922 when my father was 11 years old. Being the oldest, my father became the man of his home, responsible for taking care of his mother and younger siblings. In 1941, my father enlisted in the United States Army. After the war, he met and married my mother in 1947. In that marriage union, six boys and six girls (The Willie Dozen) were delivered by a midwife. We were raised in a four-room home without electricity, no indoor plumbing, no automobile (mules pulling wagons were our transportation), no telephone, and no television. We raised all our food (vegetables, hogs and chickens), and I attended segregated schools until the seventh grade. My discovery without my father or my mother revealing it to me was when I entered the United States Air Force in 1977, and my birth certificate was signed with the letter X, because my father could not read or write. I was not aware of his illiteracy until I entered the Air Force. That discovery moved the needle in my life, shifting my thinking about education because only six of The Willie Dozen graduated high school, and no one had completed college.

What will it take to move the needle in your life, or will your story move the needle in someone else's life? Share your story. Your own story may be the only story you need to hear to move you closer to your full potential. Ask yourself:

- **Do I see value in myself?** You must see value in yourself to add value to yourself. Denis Waitley, author of *The Winner's Edge,* attests to personal development, that you are worth the effort, time, and energy needed to develop yourself. Self-awareness is a starting point. Take an assessment to uncover blind spots and ask those in your inner circle to help you discover your blind spots.
- **Am I willing to give up to grow up?** Because I became aware of my father's illiteracy, I was willing to give up the unnecessary social activities to obtain multiple college degrees and be a positive role model for my two daughters, who became a medical doctor and a lawyer.
- **Am I a giver?** Givers, gain. Zig Ziglar once stated if you help someone get what they want, you will get what you want. I was taught that "givers, gain," by my father. After we butchered a hog, he and I would wrap pieces of meat in paper bags and walk many miles to deliver it to our neighbors. They all had much better living conditions.
- **Do I have a teachable spirit?** Initially, I struggled with being teachable. Growing up without a childhood, always working and giving lots of autonomy to my parents, I believed there wasn't anything I couldn't do within reason. I did not like someone telling me what to do. I did not care for someone challenging me. Once I became teachable, I grew exponentially. As a leadership coach, I always share with my clients; I have a coach also! I need to always be coachable.

If you see value in yourself, you are teachable. If you have a positive attitude, you are a giver. If you are willing to give up to grow up, you are attracting like-minded people. Once you know your purpose, when will you start doing what you would like to do?

ON GUARD-STAY ALERT: EYES WIDE OPEN

Lisa Bass, Major (R), Engineer, Army

*The first time someone shows you
who they are, believe them.*

-Maya Angelou

We are born with two eyes, two ears, and one mouth. There is a reason for that; to actively watch, actively listen, and then speak, which provides us with tools to construct armor for our hearts. Why address the heart? The heart exposes a person's real character and their motives. In engaging conversations or developing a new relationship, our heart should be the first thing we protect, as if we are establishing security around the CP (Command Post) in the military. The heart is our CP in the battlefield of life. Protect it! As we protect our own heart, evaluate others' hearts, as the heart displays who someone is and their purpose in your life. How is this done? It is achieved through communication, by a person's conversations, but most of all, through their actions. Remember the saying, "actions speak louder than words." Listen to someone's words as conversations occur, because what comes out of the mouth, flows the life issues. If you let someone talk long enough, they will tell you who they are. Identify their boundaries. It is not what they are willing to do, but what they will *not do at all costs* that establishes their boundaries.

Test actions against their words over time and if the words and actions line up, you are more than likely dealing with someone with good character. How do they treat people they do not need to get ahead in life? Like Chess, you position yourself for a battle; you move your pieces around the board strategically to capture the king. Yes, people play games- mind games, with actions that may appear normal to bystanders, or even the people involved, but in actuality they have concealed their counterproductive motives that will lead to well-defined and predictable outcomes. Predators have mastered this. As life is a journey, one's character is continuously developing through the experiences, trials, and tests—however, the foundation of who a person is has already been established. The key to discovering a person's foundation is through time, difficulty, communication, and actions. Therefore, it is imperative to be on guard and stay alert, with eyes wide open because it is only a matter of time before someone reveals their true self.

Here is a valuable and true adage: *It is a person's gift that gets them into a door, but their character keeps them there.*

On my first deployment to Iraq during OIF II, the war was still a new venture and the unknowns were great. We had a senior NCO (Non-Commissioned Officer) within our organization; this Soldier appeared competent, technically and tactically proficient, during all of our training events. When he spoke, it was often from a "wisdom" standpoint. I was impressed with him as a leader. I served with him for about six months during our train-up to deploy. Then that early morning came to get on the bus to depart for deployment. To our surprise, he refused to get on the bus; he refused to go. He picked the morning of our departure to take a stance for his religious belief that he was a conscientious objector. Never during our training was anything ever mentioned that he had a conflict regarding his moral or religious beliefs. The Brigade Commander gave the order to have him arrested and told the bus driver to move out, for us to catch our plane.

The NCO was later Courts-Martialed. The point being, someone can appear one way over a long period, but when tested, their real character is revealed. For the NCO, it came down to the deployment execution, and he bailed. One could speculate that he was strong in character in his faith. Maybe... however, this senior NCO knew what it takes to plan such an intense mission. He was depended on and let his Command and unit down. If he was that strong in character with his faith, then one could speculate he would have had the moral courage to stand up at the beginning of our training and make his beliefs known. He had a weak character. Salvaging an already intense morning of departure, it took our minds off what we were going into for a moment, as we pulled off in that bus in utter disbelief of what just took place. This was an extreme circumstance; however, we all have seen those types who talk the talk, crawl the crawl, and walk the walk, but when it comes time to run, they are running the other way. The bottom line: it takes time to identify the true nature and character of a person. One way to discover this is through different communication levels while testing their actions to see if it lines up with what they are communicating. Also, understanding communication levels helps you control any situation by carefully determining what to expose. Understanding communication levels is a critical technique to help one stay on guard, eyes wide open, being alert.

Through the structure of our military, some of the levels are quite clear. Serving in the military as a brotherhood and sisterhood, the objectives of these service-related conversations are more clearly defined, while other levels of communication are harder to navigate as an individual on a personal level and in the civilian world. Servicemembers already have a connection through experiences. The uniform is like a badge representing those experiences. The Combat Patch establishes another level of connection; Airborne and Air Assault wings are yet another connection. But these badges show experiences, not a person's true character and who they are. Sure, it shows that a person demonstrates the characteristic of discipline or endurance and these are admirable qualities; but it does not show you their character or motive for being so determined to accomplish their goal.

It is important to go beyond perception and identify motives and test the character. Do their actions line up with their words? As an operating principle and battle drill, test to ensure a person's actions and words line up before letting your guard down.

COMMUNICATION LEVEL STRATEGIES

As we have learned, communication is the process of exchanging information, ideas, thoughts, feelings, and emotions through speech, signals, writing, and behavior. How comfortable or close you are with someone will determine the degree of information disclosure you allow that person to have about you. The level of communication is determined by the degree of exposure and depends on the intimacy in the relationship. We learn about the components of communication, i.e. the sender and the receiver, coming up in school and training, but there is not much discussion on the actual levels of communication. The different levels identify the degree of exposure about yourself you are willing risk. Not recognizing what level you are on while speaking and what level the other person is on can lead to miscommunication, misunderstanding, and, quite frankly, in some instances, it can be dangerous. Be mindful and strategic about what level you are speaking on and on what level someone is speaking to you. Personal conversations can contain many levels of communication in any single encounter. Time tells the true character of a person; this is tested through actions and communication. You can regulate the time, ensuring there is enough to see the true character of someone, by controlling the level of communication you are allowing to take place. The shorter the time during the communication process, the higher the risk of being hurt or not seeing the truth.

A communication's level is determined by how much information is dialogued between people and what connections are perceived. The levels range from 0, which begins with the absence of existence to 5, establishing true intimacy. When you recognize that we have a natural desire for intimacy, you can better understand the battlefield in which we are operating. Through communication, we are unconsciously seeking someone to share the most inner part of our being, someone we can talk things through to make sense of life without fear or judgment. In a new relationship, we either consciously or unconsciously strive to find out what the other is seeking from us and see if it aligns with what we are looking for. The need for connection is a natural vulnerability that we all possess and should protect. It is a tendency that predators capitalize on as they move through the levels of communication. Their goal is to make you feel comfortable enough to trust them, as if they have your best interest in mind. As a result, you feel acknowledged and protected which then establishes a close connection not shared with others.

LEVEL ZERO is the absence of communication. It is the lowest level of communication where there is no acknowledgment of one's existence. It is the connection we have to the people we walk by without saying a word. It is getting on the elevator and pushing the button without even looking at whoever else is on the elevator with you. It is looking away when someone is trying to use a pickup line. It is being the lowest ranking person in a room, and no one knows you are there. Understand that in this situation, one has a job to do; if you do it and nothing negative is said.... you are good! That is just the military culture. However, a skilled leader will make everyone feel like part of the team, regardless of rank. Even if it is to say "Thank You" for setting up a meeting or conducting another aspect of a mission.

LEVEL ONE is conversation with the lowest risk of exposing yourself through words. Such discussions are without substance, but can sometimes be better than an awkward or embarrassed silence. We exchange these pleasantries by using clichés. Clichés are overused expressions that have lost the original spirit of the content or meanings. We experience this level daily with strangers and casual relationships. We do this so often; we do not even think about it. It is communication on autopilot. We communicate with those we barely know nor take the time to get to know. These phrases are heavily influenced by the setting and the respective roles and status of the parties involved. They tend to be predictable and customary, including the things we say to be polite or the things which we are expected to say. The words do not share anything between you or the other person. You offer nothing of yourself, and you expect nothing in return. You are just following the societal or cultural programmed niceties that are expected in a particular situation. This level is easy to identify for a servicemember as you walk by someone in uniform and reply with the day's greeting and/or with a salute. It can also be the casual conversation in passing as you are walking by acknowledging the other person's presence, receiving little or no response at all. It is how we treat those we see as we walk down the hallway. It is the frivolous dialogue we greet our acquaintances with that consists of the weather, the latest scores, clothes, and "hi, how are you?" to which the other person responds, "fine, how are you?" to which we reply, "fine or good." There has been no real conversation here, which makes it very hard for any relationship to develop. Although shallow, these statements are not useless because you acknowledge the other person's presence in saying such things.

I think of the movie, *We Were Soldiers, Once and Young*. In front of the School of Americas on Fort Benning, Georgia, a young SGT (Sergeant) Savage walks pass SGM (Sergeant Major) Plumley, an old crusty, no-bull crap kind of guy, and says, "good morning, Sergeant Major." The SGM replies with, "how do you know what kind of !@#!@# day it is?" SGT Savage, being startled by the response, walks on by SGM Plumley. Several days later, he again walks by SGM Plumley and greets with, "beautiful morning, Sergeant Major!" only to be furthered confused by SGM Plumley's response of, "what are you the F!@king weatherman now?" The book and movie are focused on the United States' first large-unit battle known as the Ia Drang Valley Battle of the Vietnam War. During this battle, SGT Savage's platoon becomes cut off from the rest of the unit. When the lost platoon was found after the horrific events of survival they encountered, some of the Soldiers broke down in tears of relief. Through the Grace of God, the enemy's ignorance of the lost platoon's situation, the medics first aid knowledge, the Soldier's bravery, and most important of all, Sergeant Savage's expert use of artillery fire, the platoon had incurred not a single additional casualty after SGT Savage had taken command the previous afternoon. As the survivors returned to the CP, Joe Gallaway, the reporter embedded with the unit, talked briefly to each of them and wrote, "they were like men who had come back from the dead." In the movie, SGT Savage was sitting after the rescue in utter relief when SGM Plumley walks up and says, "that's a nice day, Sergeant Savage."

From first encounters, we make impressions on others. Adhering to the old saying, "first impressions make lasting impressions." First impressions and appearances are not always accurate and need to be developed and tested over time, just as SGT Savage was confused about the impression he may have made on the SGM. Anyone with character wants to make a good impression in front of their senior leaders, as it should be. It was only over time and events that confirmed SGT Savage's true character as a Soldier to the SGM.

In some relationships, Level One is the only level couples communicate on. Their surface talk of things is said to be polite or the things that are expected to be said, including "have a good day; I love you; good night; be careful; see you later; good to see you; good morning; take care." There has been no substance to the conversation, which can strain an established relationship. On chaotic days, this may be the norm. However, if this is the relationship norm, then be very wary. If this communication remains on Level One in a relationship, it will become dull and lead to frustration and even resentment. If your partner is not sharing with you, they are more than likely sharing with someone else.

The autopilot phrases do not necessarily mean that they lack value. Level One communication allows each participant to feel a sense of safety, security, affirmation, and well-being even in a brief interaction. It serves as the foundation for deepening interpersonal relationships. Body language, facial expression, and tone of greeting confirm or deny the possible permissibility to move on to the next level later. Listening and understanding the meaning of words and clues can help you identify the transition to the next communication level.

The transition as the initial communication leads to conversations is known as Phatic Communication. It is the use of conventional messages to establish rapport, break the ice, and/or end a conversation. You might hug, kiss, shake hands, bow, smile, make eye contact, and face one another. Learn, listen, and look for the transition. Understand those clues of transitioning. Women tend to be kind, polite, and even sarcastic at times, opening the door to the next level of communication without realizing it and sometimes not wanting to. As subtle as it may be, the behavior of a person could be a clue without one knowing they are giving it. We have all seen or experienced the smooth-talking guy that a girl is not interested in; she is polite in rejecting his offer to take her out, as she smiles and slightly giggles, because she may still be flattered just the same. Unfortunately, the smile and slight giggle are clues to the guy to come back and ask tomorrow. He feels she may not be serious and is playing hard to get, and his male makeup of "loving the challenge" will have him come back and ask again. The body language is conflicting with the words.

Gestures, poses, movements, or expressions also communicate something. There is a rule of 7-38-55. In the communication process, 7% is verbal, which is conveyed through words; 38% is vocal that is received through the tone of voice, pitch, pauses, and intonations and 55% is communicated through nonverbal, which is one's body language. The body language consists of posture, gestures, facial expressions, eye contact, active movement, and physical distance. As humans, we send and interpret such signals almost entirely subconsciously. With correct leadership, our military journey is learning the ability to control our verbal and nonverbal skills. From our first encounter with the military, we are taught how Uncle Sam expects us to control our body language, from standing in Parade Rest or Attention, depending on the circumstances, to when to speak and when not to speak, and what verbal and nonverbal communication is expected. The standard is established. It is up to the leadership to expect and enforce the standard. So, stay on guard, mean what you say and say what you mean. Be aware of your actions as you are paying attention to other's actions. Our actions do speak louder than words, even in the first level of communication.

LEVEL TWO is known as "reporter talk" communication with the approach of "just give me the facts," sharing information and statistics where virtually nothing of the self is communicated. You tell me what has happened, but do not reveal how you feel about it. It is the military "BLUF" (Bottom Line Up Front) style, the way one speaks to their Commander or military leader regarding a situation or mission. In elementary school, we were taught the 4 W's: who, what, when, and where. In the military, we have the 5 W's + H, What, Who, When, Where, Why, and How. In the second communication level, people talk about topics but do not add their opinions or feelings. Although reporter talk is pretty one dimensional, it can cover a vast array of topics including what time an event starts, where you want to meet for lunch, how much a renovation project will cost, when your mother's birthday party is, to Army SPOT/SALUTE, reports to SITREPS, etc. Often, we need to convey the most important details when we do not have time to carry on a full conversation. Much of the military and life is dependent upon this kind of communication process. However, it is vital to communicate clearly when speaking on this level. There is nothing wrong with reporter talk, as long as you make an effort to go beyond this level in a personal relationship. If a couple only operates on the facts, there will be very little emotional, spiritual, intellectual, or intimate growth between partners.

During Level Two, information and statistics are shared about the weather, the office, friends, the news, and personal activities, it requires no in-depth thinking, opinions, or feelings. Gossip is included in this level, so do not confuse the fact that someone is gossiping to you that they have included you in their close circle. They are not sharing a part of themselves with you. They are revealing of themselves that if they are talking to you about someone, rest assured they are talking to someone else about you. These types of people cannot be trusted, and they have revealed a part of their character. Establish that boundary and turn away or cut off a conversation that is gossip. If you allow someone to talk to you about it, they will continue. It is not disrespectful to walk away as if having something urgent to do or politely state that you are not interested. It is establishing a boundary. Either way, the message has been sent that you are not interested in gossip. Do not worry about losing them as a "friend" because, with friends like those, who needs enemies?

We can have an ongoing, interactive relationship with someone we see repeatedly. The primary ritual within that relationship can evolve, or we can have an extended, more comprehensive interaction. We exhaust the most basic ritual forms and explore new territory while still staying within certain conversational limits and avoiding more substantive topics. This is referred to as an "extended ritual." Typical forms of extended ritual include the more variegated interactions we have with colleagues we bump into regularly or the longer conversations we have with fellow servicemembers or people we see every day. It is still "small talk," but it changes from day to day or throughout the conversation as we move through a range of unofficially sanctioned or guarded topics as one remains safe, without fear of hurting another, and with little to no risk of being misunderstood, which helps to further develop a foundation of safety and trust in the relationship.

I believe this is this area where being confident in your boundaries are most exposed. It is where people will test you to see what they can get away with during conversations. Are you confident enough to walk away from a person that gossips? Maybe you are new to a unit where there are not many females, and you want to fit in with the girls. Confidence is knowing that you can walk away, be alone and know that you will be ok. While deployed, a young female officer stated the males she had lunch with would tell dirty jokes at the table which made her feel uncomfortable. They did not tell these jokes while they were at the office, only at the lunch table. I asked her why she remained at the table. With a confused look on her face, I explained that I understood she had to work with these guys; she was trying to fit in as one of them. However, I told her that as a female serving, she will never be "one of the guys."

Finding the confidence to stand by your boundaries is hard. It is more challenging in a professional environment, even harder in a deployment environment, when you must see these people regularly with no break. But it is something that you must do; it is a must in establishing your standard of respect. That in itself gains respect. Sure, something negative may be said regarding the fact you had the confidence to stand by your convictions, but it is only because they were embarrassed. They tried to cross the line and failed. Here is the thing, sometimes there is no need for words. In the case of the jokes at the table, all she had to do was get up with her tray and sit somewhere else. That would have sent the message that their jokes were inappropriate. As a female Major, I am sure if I sat at their table, they would not have attempted to tell those jokes. The mere presence of the rank establishes the boundaries.

LEVEL THREE is the level at which we share personal ideas, judgments, and opinions. This is the level at which we step out a bit and start exposing a little of who we are as we share our thoughts. This can be a bit scary and risky as now someone can disagree with something unique to us. Risks are taken because we begin to expose our personal beliefs that can draw disagreement, hurt, and other-directed reactions. Unfortunately, this stage is put at risk when one shares such an attitude that they have no regard for what others think because they are not paying attention to the communication level stages. At this level, the simple question of, "What do you want for lunch or dinner?" opens you up to share your opinion. When one shares a new strategy or plan of action, it begins to expose your thought process. This is the level at which military missions, politics, and policies are discussed. This is how we start to know people. We share our stories and experiences. We can gauge their skills or their schedule during the previous levels, but we do not get a sense of who they really are.

This is the stage that intimacy begins to form as one begins to reveal parts of their unique selves. For the most part, women are famous for either jumping to this level quickly or confusing this level for a committed or intimate relationship. As women, we are connectors. Unless we are shy or already understand this principle of communication level, we do not recognize that we are doing this. Paying more attention by monitoring the verbal and nonverbal responses of the listener, we can gauge what level of communication the other person is on. Men are also vulnerable, just not as much. Watch as a woman communicates on this level with a man she just met. He will listen and make a few responses, but the woman will generally do all the talking. Unless the man is immediately infatuated with the woman, then her dialogue may be limited. Beware of the man's motives when he quickly jumps to this level of communication; generally, it is not in their male makeup.

Our military uniform plays a big part as it instantly establishes a connection between brothers and sisters-in-arms. Even without the uniform's presence, the second we hear active duty service or Veteran, we connect, as that bond instantly separates us from civilians. Although there may be an instant connection, as with any development of the relationship, one needs to recognize the level they are on and test before moving to the next level of communication with a person. A trigger I have discovered throughout the years is hearing the phrase, "thank you for sharing." The phrase lets me know that I shared something that potentially could move the conversation to another level; however, it was more than the other person was willing to reciprocate. It was probably unknown to them, but they let me know their boundary. At that point, I have the option to either continue to share and talk all day or pull back to the previous level. If I continue to move forward, they will not return communications on the same level nor achieve the outcome I may be anticipating. If a relationship remains at Level Three, then the person is no more than an acquaintance, as it should be until one has passed the character test to cross the line of your boundaries to enter your inner circle.

LEVEL FOUR communication consists of sharing values and feelings. What is present here is missing from Levels 0, 1, 2, and 3, which are feelings. It is easier for a woman to communicate on Level Four. We usually do not have an issue owning our feelings and being bold about it, hence our vulnerability against us if we do not protect it. A man is generally more reserved regarding his feelings and is more apt to maintain his comfort zone communicating on Level Three. Communicating on Level Four becomes riskier as it involves more intimacy. For most, it is scary to communicate on this level, as we share what we truly feel, our hopes and dreams, and who we really are, the state of our very self. It is an honor and trust atmosphere that can only be tested and developed over time and shared experiences. Revealing what keeps us going, what we are fighting for in life, and how life is affecting us is where one steps out of their safety zone if established. It is the stage when a friendship begins to share their deepest feelings and treat each other's emotions as very valuable. It is scary as our values and feelings, once shared, can essentially be used to hurt us. Someone who knows that something is important to us potentially can use it as leverage against us. This seems to be common when instant friendships are formed, and then the relationship quickly goes South. Usually, the pain of a breakup is not the absence of the other person. It is the mere fact that one shared so much of themselves that it resembles being violated or rejected.

The boundary separating Level Three from Level Four is blurry, which leads to confusion in establishing relationships. I would venture to say that this is where "crossing the line" becomes skewed in a situation. The trouble is found when one party thought there was more to the relationship, only to be blindsided with the truth that the other person was only wanting to "be friends," which is really the person saying they merely want to be acquaintances. It may be that both parties did enter Level Four, but one party did an "About Face" and went back to Level Three, while the other party failed to recognize and continue revealing their selves. One must achieve a delicate balance between Level Three and Level Four, with attention to details by genuinely listening to what the other person says while simultaneously being aware of your filters and agenda about the relationship. The technique used in the communication level strategy will assist in gauging a person's true character and agenda.

LEVEL FIVE is referred to as Peak Communication. It is the level that you can share your most inner being, your deepest darkest secrets, and fears. It is truly exposing the most vulnerable part of yourself. It is open and mutual communication that will periodically result in moments of what feels like perfect, mutual empathic understanding. This type of communication is not for everyone to hear. It is reserved for that person who is truly journeying life with you. You ultimately trust the person who would not take that information and use it against you. Some say it is reserved for your spouse or partner and God. A person who has committed to you. This level of communication is to be guarded with all your heart.

Understand that we always have feelings about something regardless of the exchange of information, analysis, problem-solving, task assignment, mission, and limited self-disclosure that comprise the bulk of Level Three conversations. When conversations on Level Four fail to achieve our communication objectives, verify first if we cannot acknowledge and express our feelings appropriately or if the other person is just not on the same level. Sometimes, it is the timing that dictates what level to communicate on. Suppose it is that time of the month, or you are completely frustrated with attempts. In that case, emotions can quickly rise to the top based on past experiences, hurts, or wounds that can generate tears if you are passionate about what you are trying to convey. For example, if finances affect a person's outlook, then the first of the month is probably not a good time to have in-depth conversations. I will go as far as to say that a full moon impacts people differently. Be aware of the external things around you. If you observe long enough, you will understand the other person's rhythm or patterns and know when to have certain conversations and what communication level to dialogue.

Finally, understand that there are three types of people that will operate in your journey of life: *Confidants, Constituents, and Comrades*. Identifying their role will assist in knowing what level of communication to dialogue within. I had the "Aha" moment, the revelation about people and their roles in our life, when I heard TD Jakes speak on this. I encourage you, regardless of your belief system, to Google "TD Jakes' Confidants, Constituents, and Comrades." Each plays a vital role in achieving your purpose in life. Most people come into your life to get you to your next destination and then leave. They were never meant to stay. Maturity is when you understand the assignment each person contributes to your life and that you do not become bitter or resentful when they depart. The distinguishing indicator for each role is the person's motive behind why they joined up with you. Over time, persons can move up, to become closer to you, or down, depending on what their *patterns of behavior* reveal. Here are the roles and their definitions:

1. **Confidants:** This is the person that comes into your life for you. To get through this life, you have to trust someone. This is the person that you can share your secrets and dreams with and know that they are safe. They will laugh, cry, agree, and disagree with you. It is the person that you can be transparent with. You can be yourself with them as if you were alone. They cheer you on in your successes and cry with you on your losses. They accept you for you, and they genuinely believe in you.

2. **Constituents:** These are the people that are with you for what you are for. Your cause, not because of you. It is about the mission. They love the mission; but don't necessarily love you. They look like a confidant. They will cheer you on. They will work with you on what you are trying to accomplish. They will motivate you and guide you in the right direction as it is the

direction they are headed toward. These people will leave you if a better opportunity comes along if it helps them in achieving their goal quicker while traveling in the same direction. These are the type of people you do not discuss your dreams and visions with as they are the ones that will take those dreams and visions and execute them for themselves. These are the people you maintain Level Three as the highest level of communication. These are the people you are generally surrounded by within your life, especially in the military. They do not leave you; they leave the mission. Servicemembers PCS or depart from the military, and you never hear from them again. Sure, you may see some on Facebook, Instagram, or other social media platforms, but the communication remains at Level Two; for the most part, they are not even a constituent anymore.

3. **Comrades:** These are the people that are against what you are against. They are fighters that have joined up with you to stand against a cause. They are the epitome of the saying, "The enemy of my enemy is my friend." This concept dates back to the 4th Century B.C. These people are powerfully driven to defeat your common enemy. These people are not for you, or your cause, it is about what you are fighting against. These people will fight by your side to victory. Most assured, they will depart from you. This is also referred to as strategic alliances. Think about it, when we go to war, this country is partnered up with other countries. This country believes in the other country because they have the same enemy, and they join forces to defeat that enemy. It is the same with people. You have been in or know someone who develops an instant friendship with someone because they did not like the third person. They rally together to discredit that third person and to build each other up. Do not get lonely and confide in these people. As soon as the alliances are finished, they are fighters; they will use what they know of you and use it against you. They are fighters. That is what they like to do.... fight, create drama. Quite frankly, I would not communicate past Level Two with this group of people.

The ironic thing is we need all three types of people in our lives to achieve our objectives. This is about being the leader of your life and understanding the many faucets of a successful journey. Do not be surprised when a relationship fails; they were the people that were meant to leave. Some people are living out their personal lives in a public place when they join up with you. Just remember they did not come to stay; they came to go. According to TD Jakes, "attitude of greatness necessitates that you do more than love when people come into your life. You have to, for your on-survival sake, get to the point you can handle when people leave." No need to become bitter, angry, or hurt; wish them well with their future. You must become a 360-degree thinker and identify the motives for each person entering your life. This key to success in interpersonal relationships is to know what level you are communicating on, and not letting the departure impact your emotions or the direction you are headed.

Most people of a certain age learn these strategies through trial and error from times when we made ourselves vulnerable, resulting in an unfavorable outcome. During our recovery, naturally, we began to build the self-defense mechanisms in our communication process without even realizing the formula behind it. We identify our boundaries regarding who we let in our inner circle. Use Levels One, Two and Three to create a foundation of safety and trust. In developing a communication strategy, seek opportunities to develop the skills necessary to sense and understand what level another person is on while managing what information you divulge. As a battle drill, walk away from conversation and assess what level you were speaking on. Question yourself and their motives so you become more strategic in your communication skill in the next encounter. If a senior leader speaks to someone of lower rank on Levels Four or Five, there is an issue there. Red flags should be flying if a senior ranking individual is talking to you on this level. It is a situation ready to go South. It is inappropriate. It is not considered disrespectful to inform them that this type of conversation is inappropriate and that you are uncomfortable engaging in it. It will set a boundary that you have made clear not to cross. If such a situation takes place, log it in a journal. This way, if there are any further attempts to cross the line, you have a recording of the appropriate steps you are taking to maintain professionalism.

The point is to test, test, test your relationships, listen to what people say and identify their motives. Pay attention to what is said to you and compare it to what is said in different environments, then ensure their actions are in line with what they say. Watch how they treat other people. Focus on the character of a person. I share this piece of advice with sincerity and as lessons learned. It is about taking a minute to stop looking through your rose-colored glasses and your interpretation of the situation that conforms to what you are desiring or needing. Observe the person at face value. Take emotions out of it and look at the facts, motives, behaviors, and communication level the other person is on without the influence of drugs or alcohol or infatuation—moving through communication levels too fast. Those things will tell you a lot about the character of the person over time. Infatuation is that intense but short-lived passion or admiration for someone, that emotion that drives you to bed with someone, only to wake up one day, look over and realize you have no clue who that person is. Setting those boundaries ahead of time by creating some basic rules for yourself can minimize later regrets. You are the Commander of your life; it is your CP that you are protecting. *On Guard, Stay Alert, Eyes Wide Open.*

A REALISTIC APPROACH

Rue Mayweather, Command Sergeant Mayweather (R), Adjutant General, Army

A man can only attain knowledge with the help of those who possess it. This must be understood from the very beginning. One must learn from him who knows.

-George Ivanovich Gurdjieff

Dear Service Member,

I am delighted that you are reading *In Her Boots*. The goal of this book is to provide relevant, smart, and meaningful information for your daily use to increase awareness of not only around you but within yourself. It is my desire that upon completion of reading this chapter of motivational wisdom from this Command Sergeant Major, you will be able to lace up your boots and stand in them, proudly exhibiting your worth.

What is self-worth and why is it important? Self-worth is the value you place on yourself. It is not what you do, but who you are. It is how you measure your self-esteem; how much you appreciate and like yourself. Self-worth is important due to the composite of your unique qualities. That is right, no one is like you. You should not compare yourself to anyone else. It arises from being shown love, appreciation, and value. It is an affirmation of being told that you are great, that you are pretty, that you can do anything, and no one is better than you. No one has told you? Then you start saying positive things about yourself! You can begin with: *I have value. I am valuable. I am worthy of all good things sent to me from the universe. I can choose to make my curses my blessings. I forgive those who hurt me. I will succeed today. My imperfections make me unique.* Surround yourself with individuals who are purpose-driven like you and intentional about their time in service, so that it will achieve much. This decision will assist in confirming the positive affirmation you tell yourself every day.

Who are you? Allow me to respond to that mystery. You are phenomenal! Yes, you are and every other lady reading this book is phenomenal. To be phenomenal is to be extraordinary, or remarkable. By chance, if you do not think those two descriptions are adequate, these words also define phenomenal: exceptional, extraordinary, remarkable, outstanding, amazing, astonishing, astounding, stunning, staggering, marvelous, magnificent, wonderful, sensational, breathtaking, miraculous, incredible, unbelievable, inconceivable, unimaginable, uncommon, unheard of. Don't you feel better about yourself?

Assign one of these saucy titles to yourself. I challenge you, when someone is trying to make you feel less than phenomenal, to straighten your back and know you are _____.

During your time in service, you may hear stereotyping remarks made like, "all Soldiers get drunk, smoke cigarettes, and cuss, and you're not any different," or, "If your mother was an alcoholic, you will be too." If you do not fit that mold, simply respond with, "I have virtue... high standards, that will be respected." Regardless if you fit the mold or not, do not become offended. Do not veer from that posture of thinking. You have every right to be you, regardless if you want to smoke, get drunk and cuss. Actions speak louder than words. You may not convince someone immediately with your words or nonverbal expressions that you do not fall into a category of stereotyping remarks, but time will tell the results of your behavior. The intent in sharing this information is for you not to put yourself in a predicament where you become an easy target for sexual assault.

According to an article in the *American Journal of Lifestyle Medicine, Sexual Violence Victimization of Women: Prevalence, Characteristics, and the Role of Public Health and Prevention*, Dr. Kathleen C. Basile and Dr. Sharon G. Smith reviewed some key factors that have shown to increase vulnerability for victimization of sexual assault. Smoking and drinking are identified as risky health behaviors linked to being victimized. So, if in fact, you do become offended to being stereotyped into a category, do not verbally respond, but take notice as to why it offended you. In fact, I would suggest that you start to journal and keep it in a safe place. Identify what was said and begin writing every thought that comes to mind that can clarify why what was said offended you. Be honest with yourself. Continue to write on the topic over a couple of days. As you mediate on it, you may discover some deep-rooted connections or feelings to what was said, that you have never identified before. Write those down. Go back and read everything you wrote. You will be surprised how writing your thoughts can assist different parts of your mind to start connecting. You begin teaching yourself about you.

Life is still one of the greatest teachers there is. The beautiful thing is you do not have to physically experience every negative situation to learn from it. The universe allows you to witness some situations from afar to give you an opportunity to say, "No that's not for me." Some of you are wise beyond your years, even at this juncture in your life. In your work environment, you may encounter someone who looks harmless. He or she is friendly, seemingly the best person you have met in the world; but they are always there each time you turn around. You do not think they are not stalking you, yet you are uncomfortable with their presence. They express uncalled for jealousy or controlling behavior over you. They try to make you think you have lost your mind by having you questioning yourself about things you know you have done and experienced in your life. This person is a Predator.

Predators look for your weak spots, whatever they are. You may not have a lot of money, or need a ride every day, or you do not have a phone. You notice when you are working, they come and try to massage your shoulders. This predator thinks you do not know what they are doing, but you are wise to their game and have told them that you hate massages. You have decided the next time the Command Sergeant Major (CSM) walks by and the predator is standing there, you are going to ask the

CSM if massages are permitted during work and what regulation can you find to support this complaint. When the answer is given, you plan to look at the predator in his eyes and say "interesting," then look back at the CSM and thank them for the information and walk off. A point will have been made. Another way to approach an uncomfortable gesture or someone touching you without your consent is just to tell them, "Stop" or "excuse me, you're in my space" or "I'd appreciate it if you didn't do that here in my area." If you mean it, do not waiver from this posture. I know finding your voice is not as easy as said. However, the confidence needed to address senior ranking personnel can be learned and developed.

Another way to prevent becoming a victim is to strengthen financial weak spots. That will keep you from being vulnerable. Having said this, make sure you have your own money. When you receive your paycheck, set up a budget for your expenses. How do you set up a budget?

Ensure you have a checking and savings account.

1) Determine the overall monthly income.
2) Determine the overall monthly expenses/bills. Expenses include a monthly deposit into your savings account, car payment and insurance as well as monthly giving to churches and charities. Write down all bills and expenses that are deducted from your pay each month.
3) Keep a record for each month's spending. After a couple of months, you will begin identifying your spending patterns.
4) Determine how much you need to live off, then save and invest the rest. This becomes more difficult if you are married or have dependent responsibilities. You still need to have a budget. However, if you are a junior service member living in the barracks there is absolutely no reason that you do not have any money at the end of the month. That behavior displays bad decisions made for your financial wellbeing.
5) Learn how to invest your money.

If you find this budget too constraining, you can always adjust it. The point being, take control over your finances. Your money allows the means to make decisions regarding your life. Having your own money builds confidence, knowing that you do not have to be dependent on someone else. This prevents a predator from thinking there is a sense of sexual entitlement attached to spending money on you or assisting you in other ways. If you have your own money, you can pay for what you need and never be put in that position.

Now let's talk leadership because leadership is important! My wisdom and experiences have taught me that a leader should possess certain qualities and virtues.

In her development, the leader has demonstrated to her subordinates that she exudes positivity, she's accountable, she's consistent in her behavior toward subordinates; she's creditable, she's trustworthy, she has integrity, she's reliable, she has proven that she is someone whom you can confide in when needed, she embraces different cultural perspectives, she's open-minded, she's committed, she's flexible, she keeps her promise, and she stands up for what is right.

A leader takes responsibility for her subordinates' successes and failures. If your subordinates see you pointing the finger and blaming them, they will lose respect for you. They will also lose respect if you take credit for something, they've done instead of giving them credit. As a leader 1) acknowledge your mistakes to your Soldiers. 2) Be transparent about the situation and be open to receiving feedback. 3) Ensure the problem is resolved and learn from these mistakes. Let your subordinates know it is alright to fail, as long as they understand the lesson learned.

Lead by example in what you do at work. It is difficult to reprimand your subordinates if you are not following the rules, procedures, or policies. Continue to develop your leadership skills. Key leadership skills which can continuously be developed are self-awareness, relational building skills, communications skills, drive and determination, resilience, confidence flexibility, vision with goal orientation, and innovation. You can learn from people around you. Do ask questions. Leaders have soft skills also known as transferable skills. These skills, such as personality traits, personal attributes, and communication skills, are needed for leaders to be successful in their job performance. Leaders gain these skills via process and development of adaptability which means they are motivated, willing to try new things, are not easily discouraged. They are innovative and creative thinkers, which means thinking outside the box. They are problem solvers and think of things no one else has considered. Do not rely on the military for the development of your leadership skills, take personal responsibility to develop them on your own.

Listen, as listening is a huge part of communication. Leaders must be able to clearly communicate to each subordinate in their organization using all forms of communication be it one-on-one, email, social media, full-staff, or other means. Being one-on-one with a subordinate allows a leader to see and hear what a subordinate says and does not say with her body posture. In other words, leaders need to be emotionally intelligent to read others emotions and know how to control their own, to not act out in anger. Leaders must develop themselves to be socially intelligent when communicating and viewing situations from other's perspectives. They listen to hear and not respond yet but learn how to solicit valuable information from her Soldiers.

Stay Curious. Curiosity is about asking questions, even if it is to yourself, and wondering why things are a certain way. I once worked for a JAG General that shared that no one on his staff ever told him anything. He later discovered was because they thought he knew everything. He would never ask anyone for help and the staff would never volunteer any information. The General realized he missed out on a lot of information and refreshing ideas. Asking "why" questions as well as "What if" and "How" questions not only allows for your subordinates to be heard and feel like they are a part of the decision-making process, but it also helps them to grow and develop into a leader.

Be intentional about your career. If you do not have a college degree or college credits, enroll in college. Check out the universities online to see what they offer. Based on the type of unit you are in; this might be very challenging based on the unit's training mission. Know that anything worth having is worth working for. Do not get discouraged if you pursue the college route and it seems that you do not have any time and your friends do. Remember, you are being "intentional" about your future. That takes both focus and commitment.

Always do your best. You will be a leader sooner than you think. Yes, you will make mistakes. We all do. The wisdom comes when you learn from what happens and you know not to repeat it. Then it's really not a loss. Ironically, I have learned that the things you fail at seem to be etched in your mind forever.

You are the next Command Sergeant Major or General. Blessings be unto you. If one perspective in this note has helped you, I too am blessed.

I leave you with these **8 *Qualities of a Wealthy Woman:***

1. **Joy -** Emotions evoked by a woman with high self-esteem, strong confidence bursting through the sun like a peacock fanning its feathers.
2. **Peace -** A place of tranquility where she is not bogged down with gossip or drama. She chooses to focus on building her business and discussing world events.
3. **Wisdom -** It is in her eyes, her soul and spirit for she has seen and felt much.
4. **Survivor -** You may not see her scars or hear about her losses, for here is a person who has failed, fainted, fallen, and gotten back up and kept moving.
5. **Rare -** She is an uncommon woman, one whom you will long remember whether it's for her leadership, sisterhood or kindred spirit.
6. **Unique -** There is only one.
7. **Essential -** Her mere existence is absolutely. She is the balance to someone's harmony and without her essentiality, there is no stability.
8. **Evergreen -** She is forever true to herself and unforgettable to all who encounter her. They may not remember her name but will remember her grace and dignity.

"You may encounter many defeats, but you must not be defeated. In fact, it may be necessary to encounter the defeats, so you can know who you are, what you can rise from, how you can still come out of it."

-Maya Angelou

RECOVERY

DON'T SUFFER IN SILENCE

Lisa Bass, Major (R), Engineer, Army

We are a summation of our life's experiences. We are shaped by both the peaks and valleys of our life.

-Wyman

What the hell just happened? Are you freaking kidding me? Did this really just happen? Shock and utter disbelief quickly set in, questioning— *Did I do something to cause this? Do I report it? Do I "suck it up and drive on?" What is my next move?* A million questions run through the mind as the heart takes over with the betrayal imprinted deeply, and the body physically exhausted, as one tries to process the traumatic event.

Wouldn't it be nice to protect yourself from everything? The military trains us on how to protect our lives and the lives of others on the battlefield. Training for these battle drills is not an option; our minds are rewired through repetition to react to a situation without a second thought. The military also trains us on how to respond to sexual assault and rape, emphasizing the reporting procedure, followed by seeking help. This is done through social media messaging, T-shirts, posters, sexual assault awareness month, and whatever other means to get the word out to report; however, it is an option, a choice. It is not a direct order on how to respond. There are several options to report and seek out help. One can choose to seek medical treatment or counseling, or report to the authority, or to file a restricted or unrestricted report; that's a lot of options to choose from when the one who has been assaulted and is in a state of confusion, lacking the courage to find their voice, wanting to crawl in a hole and continue like nothing happened. That is what I did.

I acted as if nothing happened and, in my case, bided my time for that person to leave before I felt a sense of relief. As a Lieutenant (LT) during my basic course, I volunteered to be a sponsor for the international students in our class. Although a Lieutenant, I was prior enlisted; I had been in the Army for over seven years. I had such a great experience showing the American culture to the Officers from Turkey, Africa, and the United Arab Emirates and assisting them with our Army Engineer course studies. So, when I attended my Captain's Career Course (CCC) years later, I quickly volunteered to be an international sponsor again. I was going through a divorce at the time, juggling the demands of Captain Career Course, working on my Master's Degree, raising my two children left at home, and being a grandmother all while maintaining my duties as my grandmother's guardian. She had become too ill for me to personally take care of her any longer and eventually had to be put into a nursing home states away.

I thought being a sponsor would be fun and a great distractor from being responsible, accountable, and a break from the drama from my realities. I was an older Captain (CPT), already a grandmother, but still young. I was accustomed to the work-balance concept. I entered the military as an enlisted Soldier and a single parent of three with no high school education. I had been completing my Bachelor's Degree, executing military duties, going through my Noncommissioned Officer training, and then Officer Candidate School (OCS), Airborne School as a grandmother, and attending the other required professional developmental courses executing the regular training events and field exercises. Military schools were a vacation for me - a break from the day to day responsibilities of life. So, I was excited to go to the CCC.

My classmates were great, the best group of officers I have ever served with. We were the last class to attend the Army's CAS3 course before completing our Master's Degrees, coupled with the fact that most of us were headed to the war in Iraq that had just begun. We had so many unknowns in front of us. Although there were only a few females in the class, it did not matter, we were Soldiers in the United States Army, and everyone was very supportive of each other, as it should be. We attended class daily with the weekends off.

Several times a week in the evening, after taking care of my children, who were old enough to stay alone, and ensuring they were down for the night, the international students and I would gather in one of the student's rooms in the barracks to study. We always gathered in the same male's room. Several of the international students had already developed relationships with non-military American women. Sometimes the women would hang out in the room while we conducted our studies, which made me more comfortable, as then I was not the only female in the room. After the study, we would pop a beer open, play cards, and enjoy some laughs. They became my friends. The soon-to-be-ex-husband's drama was escalating, and I would share with my newfound friends what I was going through. I needed to vent, to feel some relief as it had become too much bear alone, emotionally. Also, the drama was getting worse. They would listen and then explain how relationships operated in their culture, which I found most intriguing and exciting.

Although I was an officer in the United States Army, I was still viewed as just a "woman" in their eyes. Most of the foreign officers were around my age. I was sharing a "life matter." I felt as if I shared enough without totally exposing myself. I was not personally being judged as different cultures experience the same life situations but respond differently. I was able to talk to someone about what I was dealing with, as I was trying not to suffer in silence as friends and family members could not relate to the impacts of the divorce and my military career. Although my fellow Army Officer classmates were great, they were younger, just getting married and starting new families. I was not going to put myself in a position to be viewed as the older Officer with drama. Things happen in life, and if one has not been on that road before, one cannot expect an inexperienced person to relate and provide the needed comfort.

To look at me, one would not have known what was going on in this Officer's personal life. As much as I was trying to hold it together, unknown to myself, I did expose my vulnerabilities that would later be taken advantage of. As I mentioned earlier, "my newfound friends" is a trap that servicemembers can fall into easily...those instant relationships. We are human, and humans by nature are social creatures with a desire for companionship; even Jesus had his disciples. If you are a single servicemember or *geographical* bachelor/bachelorette and the military has assigned you somewhere away from your normal support system, this geographical situation makes the strong gravitational pull for friendships, relationships, and companionship even stronger, especially in a deployed environment. Unfortunately, this is coupled with our human desire for instant gratification, as we fail to put a person through a character test to see if they are indeed the best fit for our lives, and that's a recipe for disaster. We have our blinders on and our guard down with the basic assumption that the person or people in this newfound friendship have the same baseline and common denominator as we do, as they raised their right hand and took an oath to serve something greater than themselves. If someone tells you that they are a bachelor or bachelorette, ask them if they are a geographical bachelor/bachelorette. This term is used in the military, meaning they have a spouse residing somewhere else.

One Monday night, I showed up at the room for the study group. The international student whose room we always gathered in let me in. I sat my books on the table, grabbed a beer, and took a seat. I started looking over my notes from class and asked where everyone was that evening. He said they would arrive shortly, which seemed like a typical night, as we were discussing our notes. After about 45 minutes, he said that everyone else must not be attending. He got up and grabbed a couple more beers out of the refrigerator. He leaned over from behind me to set them on the table. He then started rubbing my shoulders, saying I was too tense. I relaxed a minute, which made it appear that I was interested. He then proceeded to kiss my neck.

I quickly shrugged my arm back to push him off to let him know that his advances were unacceptable. I find that most women in a situation with a friend or peer do find their voice, but we soften the impact of our words and actions of declined advances as we smile and giggle to make our point. It is like we are trying to make them feel comfortable as they are steadily violating our space. This strategy only invites them to continue. Our nervous smile and giggle reflect that we are not confident in what we are saying. That we are showing more regard to their feelings and the relationship than what they are trying to impose on us, giving the appearance we are not meaning what we are saying. This could lead to their defense if they did not know that is what we meant. The "gaslighting" approach of deception uses our words and actions against us, which causes us to doubt our sanity and character; they are using psychological manipulation. It is also why commanders and leadership are challenged when investigating an allegation as they are focused on the mission at hand.

He continued with his advances, so I finally got up from the table and grabbed my books. I proceeded around the table to get to the front door, where he knocked me down from behind. I was not on guard; I was not alert. I was just trying to get out of there. I was instantly pinned down and, although resisting, his strength was too much for me to handle, and I was sexually assaulted. I remember getting up in utter shock. I walked out the door and went to the elevator. As I was standing there waiting for the elevator in disbelief, he came running down the hall, saying my name. Then, he handed me this small gift bag from Victoria's Secret with sexy underwear in it; not a word was said. Then he turned around and went back to his room. I just stood there, alone in the hallway, waiting for the elevator with books in one hand and now this bag in the other. It's not that I didn't know what to do. I knew how to report. I knew where the hospital and the police station were located on post. I knew where the CQ (Charge of Quarters) for my unit was; heck, the Company Commander lived across the street from me. I knew I had no close friends at that location to call. All I knew at that point is that I wanted to get to my safe place, my home.

I drove home, drew a hot bath, sat in it, and cried. I cried for hours and finally went to bed. I was awakened by a phone call the next morning from the hospital in Alabama. My grandmother, who I had guardianship over, had been transported from her nursing home to the emergency room. The doctor was asking me whether I wanted to execute the DNR (Do Not Resuscitate) order. I knew my grandmother hated how her life had diminished to the care of others in that nursing home, and I knew how much she loved God and Lord Jesus and would rather be with them than to get better and be returned to the nursing home, so I approved the DNR. As I mentioned, my Commander lived across the street from me, so I went over and let him know what was going on. Within an hour, I received the call that my grandmother had died. She passed away on a Tuesday.

Devastated and shocked are the only two words that can describe my constant state of mind, only to be continuously plagued with utter guilt. I immediately informed my Commander. He told me to take the rest of the week off to handle the matters of her death. He could see I was distraught. That Friday, I received a phone call from that international student who assaulted me, asking how I was doing. The conversation specifically addressed my grandmother's death and when I was returning to class. Although it was a short call, I cannot explain why I took that phone call, much less fail to express my discontent with what he did to me. I later asked one of the international students' girlfriends why they did not show up that particular night. I was told that he had told them all not to come. He was clearly a predator, as he set the scene, while all the time, he was grooming me into believing he was a friend.

I did return to class the following Monday. I executed my true coping mechanism to displace myself. I have also heard this referred to as being in "zombie mode." I could not process the nightmare I was living. My schedule did not change. I did everything as before - PT, class, and yes, the study group. I did not want to bring any attention to myself. I was not my usual quick-witted and spunky self; I just functioned. I can only assume that my classmates chalked it up to the loss of my grandmother. The baths became my ritual and safe haven where I would sit and cry. I would go home at lunch and jump in the bathtub to gain some peace of mind, but in fact, my mind, spirit, and soul were so broken that I could not fathom what had become of my decision-making process. I was a Captain; I was a mother of four, two children already grown with their own lives, and already a grandmother. How could this possibly happen to me? How did I get myself into this situation? How did I allow myself to get deeper and deeper? Who was I supposed to tell that would not judge but provide comfort and understanding? I certainly wasn't going to share it with someone younger than me that had no clue about life or having two children still needing to be taken care of while going through a divorce. I was broken, ashamed, embarrassed, and humiliated. My vulnerabilities were exposed and taken advantage of. It seemed like my case was one drama situation after another to the point of no return. My career was the only thing I had to hold onto to have some sense of control and success in my life.

An article published by the PCAR (Pennsylvania Coalition Against Rape), titled *Common Victim Behaviors of Survivors of Sexual Abuse*, states that "offenders reinforce negative feelings by the things they say and do to their victims. The offenders use shame and fear to bind their victims and isolate them from others who might help them. Though it may be difficult for one to understand, many victims continue to have a relationship with their abuser."

I will interject and emphasize the importance of not judging people too quickly; individuals react differently to trauma. It is a situation that one does not know how they will respond until faced with that exact situation. One does not know what another person has been through in their life that is a driving force in their decision-making process. With that said, people with life experiences can identify the impacts of a decision. A person with wisdom can usually point out what is driving the decision while also recognizing the consequences.

Regardless, if you have experience or wisdom or are just a bystander, *don't judge too quickly* as you are not "in her boots" with all the circumstances from past to present that impact their behavioral outcome. Compassion is all that is needed and what one should expect in this situation. The article continues to say, "it is common for victims to maintain contact with their abusers because they may feel affection for them even though they hate the abuse. This is especially normal when the abuser is a member of the family or close friend." This statement is profound to me. As horrible as MST is, the fact that a brother or sister-in-arms wearing the uniform brings harm to a fellow servicemember, essentially has the same impact as if it were a blood relative; these are the very people that you are trained to trust to have your six on the battlefield.

It is also common for some victims to maintain contact to regain control over their assault. Others may maintain contact to regain a feeling of normalcy. The bottom line is not to make assumptions about how you think a victim should react. We cannot say how we would immediately react if found in a similar situation. While deployed to Iraq, a female SGM, who is part of the *In Her Boots* team, spoke about how to react in these situations after finding herself going through such an experience. She had walked into her CHU (Containerized Housing Unit), laid her weapon on her bed and walked across the room to her locker, which was directly across from the opening of her door. She didn't realize that she had forgotten to lock her door until it was too late. Suddenly the door flew open and there stood a male Soldier from Uganda. She froze, and he froze. He was at the wrong CHU and meant no harm. However, all this time in her mind, she knew how she would react to a situation, especially being armed with a 9-millimeter pistol; but there she stood, unable to move, paralyzed and confused.

The point here is, we may think we know how we will act, especially if we are trained, as we are in the military, but the truth of the matter is, until we are in a situation and faced with all the circumstances, we do not know how we will respond. Please do not ask questions like "why were you there?" or "why did you stay?" to try to make sense of it for your peace of mind. It does not matter what the situation was or how it evolved to turn you into a victim. If a person is a victim, another person should show compassion and help guide them while they are in their dark place, back to light.

I thought my strategy would be the classic Army "suck it up and drive on," that there were only a couple of months left in completing CCC and this man would go back to his country, and I could dismiss in my mind that this had ever happened to me, but it did not work out that way. The sexual abuse continued, and mental and physical violence came with it. His threats of violence were only solidified as this man would tell his war stories and his killings during class and reiterate them during the study group as to how many people he had killed and in the manner in which he did it, enough details to strike fear in anyone not to tangle with him. As I write this, I think, "what was I thinking; why didn't I get help?" The truth of the matter is I was scared for my life. The mere fact that he had a clear conscience after killing only incited a fear in me I had never known. This guy was from another country. I had studied the wars of his country; I knew what atrocities had taken place. A combination of fearful emotions, matters with my divorce, and my mind not in the right working order to process the whole situation left me virtually paralyzed to do anything, but to exist one day at a time.

The physical abuse, leaving bruises on my arms, sent me back to my teenage years, as I was raised in an abusive environment. All those coping skills I learned as an adult and my military training as a Non-commissioned Officer and Officer flew right out the door. I was in fear for my life, my children's lives, and my career. Everything I worked my whole life to accomplish, I thought, would be gone in a flash. So, I stuck it out, I went through, enduring what this man dished out for months until that day he stepped on the plane and flew out of this country. Here is the honest, twisted part that this type of abuse can have on one's physiological state of mind. I did not realize how much control over my life he had taken, or I had given away. The truth is, I did not know what to do when he left. There was an empty void and a degree of rejection as he had been in almost every second of my day. If he was not right next to me in the classroom environment, he surely was always watching and lurking in the background. He was in control. Although relieved, his departure revealed my thought process, that I was just tossed away like a piece of trash.

As I was still going through my divorce, my soon-to-be ex-husband called the CG (Commanding General) of the post and reported that one of his Officers, identifying me by name, had committed adultery. I was told to report to the Battalion Commander immediately. I was forced back into reality and in full defense mode, in the protection of my career. I have to say, I learned something from my Battalion Commander that day on how to handle a situation. His questioning was so strategic that he did not allow me to compromise my integrity while maintaining the facts of the issues that needed to be addressed. He did not put me in a position to give out any information that I did not want him to know. He addressed the issue that was brought before the CG but never questioned me directly on the allegation of adultery; he just reiterated what had been said. He then shifted the focus to my divorce proceedings status and where I was in the process. I explained all the legal measures I had taken to finalize with no resolve.

The truth of the matter is, I was in such a "shut down mode" I could not handle anything but getting up out of bed, taking care of my kids, and completing the course that I was in. I was steadily falling behind in completing my Master's Degree that the Army gave me the opportunity to obtain, and that the Engineer Corp expected their Officers to have. It was too difficult for me to concentrate. The additional looming fact of the war in Iraq ramping up was almost too much for me to bear. I had the lingering question of, "if I get notification of deployment, what was I going to do with my children?" as I did not want them to go to my soon-to-be ex-husband, but that potential was in the future, and I needed to deal with the present. As I explained to my Battalion Commander what I had done concerning the divorce, he looked at me and said, "you are a Commissioned Officer in the United States Army, and I expect you, as an Officer, to get off the defense and move into the offense!" His stern voice was so powerful that it sent shock waves through me. He reminded me of who I was. I was not a victim of any circumstance; I was a leader, and I was in control of what needed to be done and had the skillset to handle the situation in front of me.

Looking back now, I only handled the circumstantial things, like all the paperwork and dealing with the divorce attorney and going through the court process. I did what I needed to do to move forward; however, I still was not present for all of it. Being "present" required me to become vulnerable, to deal with my wounded mind, spirit, thoughts, and emotions. I did not know how to do that. I was not wholeheartedly involved in my own life, and for that, I realize I missed a lot, especially with my children. As Soldiers, we know this type of behavior. We "dismiss" ourselves as we are going through things, that zombie mode, a mechanism we often use when we show up for PT in the morning. We hit the alarm clock; we make it to the formation, but we are not engaged in those push-ups, sit-ups, or the run. We "checked the block" for accountability, but we dismissed the opportunity for that day to develop our bodies with every bit of energy for that next PT test. If this behavior continues at each PT session, it is accurately reflected on the PT test. Guess what? Suppose one dismisses an event and does not receive the appropriate skills for the process. In that case, it shows up in the choices and decisions made that impact their lives and continues to impact their lives until that person finally stops, addresses, and seeks help with the issue. It will eventually show up somewhere in life, just as executing in zombie mode in PT sessions will be reflected on a PT test.

If you are young, most likely you have not experienced that pivotal point when you are, as they say, "brought to your knees." This is that point when life appears to be crashing in, and you do not know why, so you bow down and look up to the heavens, because "your way" has not worked. It would be nice to tell you that everyone is immune to this state of mind, but it is not true. Everyone will come to some point in life where something so devastating happens that the body automatically goes into an instant survival mode. It becomes blinded to the facts, as is said, "one cannot see the trees from the forest." As harsh as it may seem, it is reality; it is life. The Veteran population is experiencing this to the degree that on average, 22 veterans commit suicide a day. Once you leave active duty, there are enough challenges just trying to reintegrate back into the civilian world as a Veteran. Arm yourself with as much of the healing process and coping skill sets before you leave the military as you possibly can. Suppose you do not want to use the active duty resources. In that case, there are nonprofit organizations within your area, regardless of where you are located, that you can reach out to for assistance, and the information will not be shared with your Chain of Command.

If you have been victimized, please do not do what I did and suffer in silence by trying to dismiss it. It took many years, but I finally had to come to terms with what happened. I had a very successful military career because that is all I focused on. Years later, I finally completed my Master's Degree as that was a 300-meter target when I was only capable of shooting my 25-meter target during that turbulent time, and it cost me a promotion. Once I completed the degree and submitted it to my records with nothing else, I was number three on the next Army promotion list. It did not matter how good I was at my job or deployments. The mere fact that I did not complete what was required for an Engineer Major, the Master's Degree, caused me to suffer for a year. Back then, I could not focus; the missions were enough to keep me distracted from what I needed to do...sit down, focus, and complete the assignments for my Master's Degree. Besides avoiding what I knew I needed to do to get promoted, other impacts of suffering in silence that were clearly from my choices surfaced when I retired. Once a person leaves the military, they are left with... life. There is no mission or leadership to provide purpose, motivation, and direction. There is no promotion to strive for to distract you from your reality. One quickly finds themselves facing the aftermath of not getting the appropriate assistance to navigate the healing process.

It is so important to be authentic, open and true to oneself, to walk out your journey alone for a while, to get to know who you are, your own vulnerabilities, without validation from anyone or to let anyone become a distraction when dealing with the situation you have been subconsciously trying to avoid. This is not to be confused with isolation. Isolation is a dangerous thing; your thoughts can quickly turn negative. One still needs to surround themselves with safe and healthy people for comfort and encouragement. "A person left to themselves will inevitably self-destruct." You may be nodding your head, thinking, *I have heard this before, or I am already doing this*. I had heard it before also, but somehow it did not resonate with me on a practical application level when it applied to me. I concluded that I had information, which we all do, and I understood it. But I did not have the actual understanding of these basic principles or training on MST until I was forced to face the aftermath of destruction in my own life. When I had to walk a season of silence, I dug deep and dealt with many unresolved traumas. In counseling, I addressed many issues that made me uncomfortable inside. However, I did not stop going even though I did not always like what I heard or what the mirror was reflecting back at me. It was in those uncomfortable times that I truly healed, grew and became a better version of myself. In addition to doing the hard work, I journaled. At times, I felt as if I was having a brain overload as I tried to process everything. Stopping to freely write my thoughts down allowed me to introspectively examine my life and the situation in which I found myself. The process of writing things down on paper cleared my mind. Journaling helped me examine my patterns, triggers, and identify things I never realized about myself. It helped me develop a relationship with myself. Now, I understand my vulnerabilities; when attacks from the enemy come, and they will come, I understand what is going on and react differently, which produces positive results, not a reaction that will cause me to continue an old, dysfunctional cycle of regrets. Most importantly, I learned to forgive, not only him but myself, and let go.

As of today, more and more women in the military are *Finding Their Voice.* They are reporting and standing strong through the Courts-Martial process. However, there are still sisters-in-arms that choose to "suffer in silence" and continue in life as if an MST event did not occur. They are employing the "suck it up and drive on" concept. The trauma is too much to bear, coupled with going through the medical and Courts-Martial process's scrutiny and the perceived impacts on their career, unit morale, and personal life. I admire those women who see their accused come to justice, to endure the fight in court that can exhaust the last bit of resource within their emotional, mental and physical state of being. Seeking out justice is only part of the process; one must seek additional help to recover from mental and emotional wounds. Without going through the necessary steps for recovery from the actual trauma and regaining strength, harmful coping mechanisms gradually and unsuspectingly develop, affecting the choices, decisions, and quality of life. Dealing with MST by acknowledging what has happened, and accepting that it has happened, and deciding to go through a recovery process are the first steps to healing. Significant efforts are a must in taking care of you in the aftermath, to move from an MST Victim, becoming an MST Survivor, to being an MST Thriver!

The end state of the recovery process will never undo what has been done. If MST has taken place, understand that it does change you, but it does not reduce you, and most certainly, it does not define you.

TAKING CARE OF YOURSELF IN THE AFTERMATH

Lisa Bass, Major (R), Engineer, Army

Accept yourself, love yourself, and keep moving forward.
If you want to fly, you have to give up what weighs you down.

-Roy T. Bennett

As with everything, recovery is a process, regardless of what hurts or pains you have suffered. The fact is you will not get through this life unscathed, either from your own doing or at the hands or decisions of someone else. That leaves you with a choice: you can choose to remain to suffer and survive, or you can choose to heal and live, not just exist in your life. What does recovery mean? According to the Merriam-Webster dictionary, the definition of recovery is "the act or process of becoming healthy after an illness or injury; the act or process of returning to a normal state after a period of difficulty." To act is to take action and do something. A process is a series of actions or steps taken to achieve a particular end. A process gives you depth, strengthens your roots, and builds character. It appears in today's society that everyone wants promotion without the process. Face it, "Life is a Process." Understanding this concept and approaching every situation with this concept in mind will reduce stress and conflict with others and within ourselves.

The recovery process can begin when the woman chooses to recover and is honest with herself to not remain in a state of being a victim or survivor. A decision and commitment are made to take the necessary steps to achieve a healthy and thriving lifestyle once again. Recovery removes the words of "victim" and "survivor" from one's mind's imprint. She recognizes herself only as a "thriver," a happy, confident, and productive individual who believes that she has a prosperous life ahead. She is primed to follow her dreams! Regardless of whether it is making the military a career, finding a new job, going back to school, starting her own business, writing her story, or staying at home and dedicating her life to her family, the choices are limitless.

thriver:
a healthy, happy person with a brilliant, productive future.

A choice is an option between two or more possibilities. A choice resonates in the mind as if you still have the other option available, whereas a decision is aimed at an outcome; it puts death to the other options. It is a decisive action to produce a definite result. Think about it this way: in any military mission, there are planning steps involved. During the planning phase, there are choices to be made, in the Army, this is referred to as Courses of Action (COA). The servicemember can make choices regarding a mission, but when the Commander gives that direct order, which may be verbal or a written decision, then all of the choices become invalid compared to the decision of the Higher Command and delivered as an order. Think of a decision as a direct order to your mind! Half the battle we face is making a decision in our life, but once the decision is made, the stress from indecisiveness is removed.

As the *Commander of Your Mind*, give yourself a direct order. You may not know exactly where the path may take, but at least you have a direction. As simple as making a decision may appear, it is one of the most challenging things to accomplish. Writing this process in a formula looks like: *Decision + Execution = End State*. Looking at it this way prompts a servicemember to say, "too easy, Drill Sergeant!" However, it is one of the hardest things a person does in living their lives. It is ownership of the outcome.

Have you ever noticed that an outsider with an ounce of experience can look at a situation, sum it up, and give suggestions that on the surface appear so easy? It is not the case when you are "in it." When a person is "in it" and the pain is so great, the mere choice of something can bring one to pure exhaustion. Most of the time, a person in pain cannot hear others trying to advise and guide them, much less make a decision. "Their thinking ain't right," as one may say. Unfortunately, without decision and direction, one essentially just exists and floats through life without really living.

I despise the statement, "time heals all wounds." Time does not heal all wounds. Time is the period in which a process occurs for a person to go through to heal properly. However, time can be your best friend. Imagine a cut on your arm. Initially, the wound heals enough for a scab to form and cover the wound. If that scab is bumped off, it will begin to bleed again. It is the healing process in which the wound becomes a scar, not time. The scar will always remain. It just will not hurt anymore. Once healed from being a victim, the scar hopefully becomes a reminder of the knowledge gained to display patience and humility for others going through a similar process. The mere understanding of the need to have compassion will be the mechanism to help someone else, especially during their "zombie mode" in the event of an assault or other traumatizing event.

To "suffer in silence" can be identifiable as it becomes a continuous cycle or pattern that seems to prevent you from moving forward. It keeps you in survival mode regardless of how hard you try, leaving you to think, "I am trying to make the right decisions; why does this stuff continue to keep happening?" It is the process that heals the wounds, not time.

Servicemembers trust their leadership because their rank, for the most part, establishes that they have been through a process; they are grounded; they are knowledgeable, and their experience is to be trusted. Seek out that person who has been faced with a similar situation and made it through. Although we are created for something special in life, I guarantee you that someone else has had a similar experience. Even though it appears that another sister-in-arms has not, you may be surprised. Yes, it is harder to find the one you may need to help you through, but she is out there. I give a lot of credit to the sisters-in-arms that have created Facebook pages that allows the fellow sisters to reach out to one another in a private message to seek additional advice or guidance; but this is only a support mechanism, not qualified help for recovery. If you are a friend, peer, or superior, take the initiative to seek out an actual counselor or program for sexual assault recovery for a person who has been inflicted. The recovery assistance should not be confused with a victim advocate's duties and responsibilities in the unit or a buddy; they are added support. The real healing comes from doing the work needed under the guidance of someone who is qualified.

You have access to a Vet Center near you that can provide support with qualified personnel. Help does not have to come from the active duty military service community; there are Veteran services off post or base. These free services are for Veterans and active duty, Reserves, and National Guard. Granted, many of these Vet Centers are staffed with male retired Veterans, often from the Vietnam War era who are not as familiar with female servicemember experiences. However, that should not be a deterrent for getting the help you are entitled to. If you are ever faced with this situation, you can demand to have a female counselor, which the VA is responsible to provide. They will have a female counselor made available in your area through travel arrangements. If you do not feel comfortable or cannot connect with the counselor you've been given, such as knowing that they are present with you, ask for another counselor. Essentially, if you are not comfortable with things conveyed, then you are not healing and growing. This is not about the counselor agreeing with everything you think. That is what so-called friends are for, because a real friend, mentor, or counselor will correct you when headed down a wrong path. Do not assume everyone is out there to help. Unfortunately, some are just collecting a paycheck, but do not let that hinder you in your recovery process. Identify it for what it is, make a complaint if needed, and move on. This is your life, and you are the Commander of it.

Regardless of the form of MST, it impacts the soul (will, mind, and emotions), body, and spirit. The fact that the military culture is based on a rank structure lends to a predator's playground of subordinates. On the other side of the spectrum is the human relationship factor and not understanding how to identify and communicate appropriate boundaries. However, if you find yourself in a situation, know and understand what to do next for the care of you. Know how to care for a friend and care for a subordinate if you are the one first called for help. Since 2010, during the incorporation of the TF SASA (Sisterhood Against Sexual Assault) and the *In Her Boots* program in Iraq, the Department of Defense has taken measures to respond to MST cases through the legal proceedings and discharge methods. The military informs everyone how to report with their flyers on boards and once a year "Death by PowerPoint" training. One has the right, with an emphasis on responsibility, to report abuse. Standard military training provides options, and they explain what to expect if one does or does not decide to report.

They stress that sensitive and knowledgeable support without bias for the victim is the standard during the criminal justice system. The fact is that going through the Courts-Martial proceeding can be brutal, like being raped or assaulted all over again. It may not come from one particular thing. Just the process alone is a fight within itself. It is a procedure full of drama where the defense attorney's cross-examination has an impact on a victim's soul. One may or may not have the support from their unit or Chain of Command and are victimized again or even worse, as they are left to feel as if they are in solitary confinement and alone, regardless of how many people are around. Chances are, if one has been victimized before, either as a child, teen or as an adult, and did not report or seek help for healing then, they are most likely to continue to "suffer in silence," and the cycle of coping as learned helplessness is continued.

SEEK MEDICAL ASSISTANCE, REGARDLESS

Regardless of how one chooses to report or not report, seek medical attention! It is your personal decision regarding who else should be told about what happened. You have a right to privacy, but you must seek help to get the proper care to recover fully. Granted, seeking medical assistance is not the first thing that comes to mind during an assault unless the person is physically abused to the point that it demands medical attention. Complicating the situation further is the underlining stigma one may feel after an assault. No Commander wants to deal with an assault case within their unit. It distracts from the ongoing mission and destroys unit morale, which is the military priority. A victim may not report due to fear about not being believed, worried about the impact on their career, and fear of retribution. If assaulted, the unknown of what will happen during the process of seeking medical attention only adds weight to anxiety and emotional instability a person may feel— explaining ahead of time what to expect can provide some comfort and confidence in taking the right steps. Regardless of where you are located, each location has a SANE (Sexual Assault Nurse Examiner), either in the ER, OBGYN, or a hospital clinic and is on call 24 hours a day and seven days a week. Even deployed, there is access to a SANE.

The Sexual Assault Nurse Examiner's purpose is to meet the victim's immediate needs by providing compassionate, culturally sensitive, and comprehensive forensic evaluation and treatment. The objective is to offer a warm, comfortable environment, not the imagined cold, sterile environment where a victim is treated like a slab of meat on a steel table. The nurse is registered and has advanced education in forensic examination and truly understands how fragile the situation is. The SANE program's objectives are to protect the victim from further harm, provide crisis intervention, provide timely, thorough, and professional forensic evidence collection, documentation, and preservation of evidence, evaluate, and treat prophylactically for Sexually Transmitted Diseases (STDs).

They also evaluate pregnancy risk, offer prevention, assess, document, and care for injuries. These nurses appropriately refer victims for immediate and follow up medical care and counseling, and enhance law enforcement agencies' ability to obtain evidence and successfully prosecute sexual assault cases. The advantage of a SANE examination is that it provides a higher standard of evidence collection. The care can speed the victim's recovery to a higher functioning level and prevent secondary injury or illness. It ultimately increases the prosecution of a sex offender and reduces the chances of another incident or rape. This part of the process arms Judge Advocate Generals in their effort to combat sexual assault in the military, if the victim chooses to disclose.

In a state of shock after an incident, one is rarely thinking if they want to report or not. I will venture to say, the mere thought of going from a negative situation into another is not at the top of the list as a coping strategy. Fear, guilt, and embarrassment sometimes make it difficult to report and tell others closest to you. If you find yourself in this God-forbidden situation, do not cut off your options and choose to suffer in silence. You may not want to legally report at the moment, however, the best time to collect evidence is immediately after the incident. A report is made during an examination, a consent form is signed, and a complete and thorough evaluation of care and evidentiary exam is conducted. During the forensics collection, the SANE will swab for seminal fluid, gather hair combings, and collect saliva from the mouth as DNA evidence can be collected from any kissing and/or licking and from identifying any stains on all clothing. Blood will be drawn for pregnancy, HIV, and STD testing. Defecation samples may also be collected if needed. An alcohol and drug test will be performed, and photos taken. The SANE will document any genital and non-genital injuries. After the forensic collection is performed, all evidence is labeled and placed in an envelope, sealed, signed, and secured. SANE provides the types of evidence collected in rape cases to agencies to use as evidence if you choose. They determine the source of specimens and maintain the chain of evidence while adhering to the evidentiary exam timing and protocol. SANE is responsible for providing the documentation and recordings with a jury in mind, while their evidence can also be used for testifying in court as an expert witness and factual witness. Only with your consent may the evidence be turned over to the police; otherwise, the evidence can be held up to five years while you decide if you want to pursue a criminal investigation.

In order to assist SANE in evidence collection, it is best that the victim does not shower, brush their teeth, urinate, eat, drink or change clothes and goes directly to the location of a SANE in their area. Although an exam can be conducted up to five days after an assault, evidence can be lost by delaying, especially if the victim has showered or done any of the things on the list. Understandably, the first thing that a victim wants to do is take a shower or bath, "to wash it all away." Please seek medical assistance and help others not to be in the same situation with the assailant. Other things that SANE will need to know are the activities of the victim that may have destroyed evidence, like changing clothes, bathing, douching or bowel movement, and tampon use, if there has been any consenting sex within the last 72 hours and with whom, what type or any contraceptive use, if currently pregnant and if the victim has any allergies. After the examination, the victim will be allowed to shower, brush their teeth, and change clothes. If needed, medication will be prescribed, and a medical follow-up scheduled.

We cannot say how we would immediately react if found in a traumatic situation. We may think we know how we will respond, especially with all our military training. But the truth of the matter is, until we are in a situation and faced with all the variables in one's life, we do not know how we will respond. Decide now, as a battle drill, that medical assistance will be sought immediately in the event of an aftermath. Identify now who you would call and where you would need to go.

SIGNS OF EMOTIONAL AND PHYSICAL REACTIONS TO TRAUMA

A traumatic event such as MST can leave a victim with raw emotions, feeling vulnerable, and losing control over their environment coupled with actual physical pain from the trauma itself. Therefore, it is important to know yourself and recognize the signs and symptoms of the trauma on your emotional and physical being. As a leader, it is essential to know your servicemembers as you are responsible to identify emotional and behavioral changes. Also, pay attention to the symptoms that are written on the sick call slips as they could be indicative of trauma that is not being addressed.

Granted, everyone processes an event differently depending on their background and individual makeup. However, when the body has experienced a traumatic event, it will generate an automatic response that the individual cannot control. Some common reactions to MST are avoidance of people, a feeling something is missing or is not right, depressive symptoms, alcohol and or substance abuse, suicidal thoughts, shattering of previously held beliefs, self-blame and shame, trust issues, outbursts and controlling issues or promiscuous behavior to avoid depression.

Other common reactions to be aware of after a sexual trauma include nonspecific health problems and somatic complaints such as those symptoms that have no medical explanation. One will experience the emotional reactions that make you feel like you want to avoid people, places, and things related to the event. A person may easily become upset, agitated, and irritable, or have outbursts of anger. Most likely, they will feel nervous, helpless, fearful, and/or sad. It is the body and mind in defense mode to self-protect with negative consequences.

There are five common stages that a victim will begin to progress through while experiencing the emotional and physical reactions to trauma. The common stages after a sexual assault include initial shock, denial, reactivation, anger, and integration with the appropriate guidance or counseling. The stages are like the five stages of grief, including denial, anger, bargaining, depression, and acceptance. However, without help, someone can become stuck in a stage (most commonly the anger stage), without properly healing and carrying on with a beautiful life that waits ahead.

If you are in this unfortunate position and feel like a train wreck, understand this is a normal reaction to a traumatic event and that you are going to be ok. Granted, if you allow yourself to do the hard work and go through the complete healing process, the once traumatic event will become a faded memory, with only a scar as a slight reminder. It is essential to understand that sexual assault does change you, but it does not reduce you, and most certainly, it does not define you.

Below is an outline of the battleground landscape one faces during the aftermath of a sexual trauma without choice. The "suffer in silence" tactic that impacts the continuous cycle or patterns that become recurring in one's life seems to prevent women from moving forward. Regardless of how hard one tries, in the survival mode, one asks themselves, "I am trying to make the right decisions; why does this stuff continue to keep happening?" It is usually a reflection of the vulnerability of being stuck in a stage. Information and understanding of the stages provide a foundation. However, when the revelation of what is taking place in the aftermath is understood, the healing can begin.

STAGE ONE is initial shock. As I've said, I like to refer to this as the "zombie mode." It is the stage that includes a feeling of shock, numbness, and being unable to feel love or joy; it's the instant coping mechanism before the brain can process the experience. As you replay the events in your mind, shame can creep in along with blaming yourself or having a negative view of oneself or the world. During this state of high alert, self-protection leads to a distrust of others, even getting into conflicts and being over-controlling. I heard someone say that trying to control their environment was like a dysfunctional way of attempting to gain control over their feelings; and it does not work. Being withdrawn, feeling rejected or abandoned is also normal, along with losing intimacy or feeling detached. It is normal for physical reactions to appear such as an upset stomach, eating excessively, or loss of appetite, trouble sleeping, nightmares and feeling very tired, pounding heart, rapid breathing, feeling edgy, easily startled, having suicidal thoughts, feeling confused and irritable, and having flashbacks of the event. Other physical reactions may include experiencing severe headaches if thinking of the event, memory loss, and failure to engage in exercise, diet, safe sex, regular health care, and neglecting other medical problems. A victim may mask their pain with unhealthy coping strategies such as excessive smoking, alcohol or drug use, compulsive shopping, and sexual activities, along with other poor choices and decisions.

STAGE TWO is denial. This is when a victim experiences a period of "pseudo-adjustment." The victim functions on a superficial and practical level by resuming life activities, while feeling isolated, intermittently depressed, and exhibiting mild PTSD symptoms. While on active duty, this is so easy to do. The distractor of the unit's mission and physical activities can occupy the mind and body, especially if one is deployed. Disbelief that the event ever occurred can be a form of protection from the overwhelming feelings associated with the trauma. The mind is a powerful thing and can refuse to acknowledge and process an event.

STAGE THREE is reactivation. It involves re-experiencing the feelings from Stage One, as if "life has fallen apart," usually brought on by something that triggers memories of the assault. The symptoms may be more prevalent for others to see in your personal life than your professional life, as you are no longer in "zombie mode" and the feelings seem to be more prominent. It may be the first time you decide to share what has happened to you. Those who you previously shared the event with may be confused, as they thought you had recovered from the trauma, when in fact, you were in one of the earlier stages. The anxiety and fear of future assaults may cause you to isolate yourself, as depression, shame, hopelessness, and self-doubt may quickly set in. You may experience nightmares or night terrors, flashbacks, and have feelings of vulnerability. There may appear to be more academic or relationship difficulties. The tendency to blame yourself for the assault can be the most destructive feeling during this stage. Do not blame yourself! Those moments of questioning if you were in the wrong place, if you should have known, what could you have done differently, or self-guilt if alcohol was involved, are just negative thoughts not to be entertained. But these thoughts attack the mind furiously.

Come up with a positive saying to repeat out loud when these thoughts occur. Speaking out loud every time a negative thought enters your mind will eventually be replaced by remapping your thought pattern. Be the Commander of your mind. I go one step further with a physical motion by flicking my fingers on my right hand as if I were flicking a piece of lint off my clothes. I use all aspects of my being to arm myself and change the negative thought pattern through my soul, body, and spirit. So, for me, I flick my fingers and say out loud, "Get Off Me!" without hesitation; I follow with, "I am the Righteous in God, through Jesus Christ who loves me!" It would immediately bring peace to my state of being. You choose your own, but I highly suggest targeting the soul, body, and spirit to guard against anything negative coming into your space. The mind cannot process two thoughts simultaneously, so changing the thought pattern, coupled with a physical motion, immediately blocks those negative thoughts. The mind is the battleground in this stage. The bottom line is no one deserves to be assaulted, so it does not matter where you were or what you were doing. If it was unwanted, then that is it. Nothing else changes that fact!

STAGE FOUR is anger. Anger is an instinctive, natural way to respond to threats or perceived threats. But when it gets out of control by expression or suppression and turns destructive, it can lead to problems at work, personal relationships, and overall quality of life. Feelings of anger can be healthy when those feelings are directed toward the assailant. Unfortunately, this feeling of anger can be misdirected toward yourself, friends, significant others, society, the military, the Chain of Command, the legal system, all men or women, etc. The reality of the situation is nothing can undo what has been done. That produces anger, only to be fueled with the feeling of not having any control. With skillful support and professional help, this anger can be redirected in ways that are healing. It is ok to get angry; you need to get angry. Be honest with yourself and others that you are angry at what has happened to you. If you feel as if you cannot control your anger by responding to things in an assertive manner, then let it out in a safe environment. Get mad, scream, cry into your pillow, yell it out to the heaven above, experience your feelings, and let the boiling point of the anger be released in private and not directed at others.

The anger can cleanse your spirit as it indicates you are beginning to integrate the event into your life and move on without guilt. Unfortunately, this, too, is a stage that one can become stuck in. As anger can quickly turn into bitterness, poison to the heart blows out the candle of joy and leaves the soul in darkness. If stuck here, you can function in society, pretty much punching the card of life, not finding true, healthy happiness. It is likely the suppressed anger was turned inward, then converted or redirected. It happens when you hold it in, stop thinking about it, and focus on something positive. You may even become very successful in your career or financial status. You are a survivor of the event. Life will continue to circle without ever really making progress, riding a rollercoaster of highs and lows. The suppression may reveal itself in overachievement, igniting the feeling of constantly doing something to overcompensate or distract from the hidden anger and pain. But do not be fooled; what is kept in the dark will eventually come to light. As the suppressed anger becomes the norm, it may eventually reflect in your health as hypertension, high blood pressure, or depression.

When a survivor comes to terms with their anger and acknowledges that they had no control over what happened and were not to blame, they may begin to re-experience the intense feeling of anger, along with fear and rage. This may be directed toward everyone except for their assailant because the assailant is the "least safe target" for the victim's anger. During this stage, it is common and healthy to begin the grieving process, start to face the pain, and learn how to forgive, not only the assailant but yourself. There are many books on the market, such as "Healing the Wounds of the Past" by TD. Jakes; "Enemies of the Heart" by Andy Stanley; and my favorite, the Bible which I like to refer as "Basic Instructions Before Leaving Earth," regarding the grieving process and the impacts it has. They are well worth the investment to purchase, to gain information, understanding and revelation about this process. There is ample information on the internet, just Google "grieving processes." In the military, we are at a higher risk to endure tragedies and death of our brother and sisters-in-arms. We cannot be sheltered from the grief we experience, regardless of if we talk about it or not. It is a clear indicator with the Veteran suicide rates, that the grieving process is not addressed in the day-to-day operations while on active duty. That is considered a mental health issue and not military operations. Be a leader of yourself, Commander of your mind and seek out the resources.

STAGE FIVE is integration. This is the most challenging and joyful stage for complete recovery. It is the stage when you accept what has happened as part of your life's experience and journey. A sign you are in this stage is thinking and talking about it does not send you back to one of those previous stages. You may still have some fears regarding your safety, anxiety, and memories, but for the most part, these subside. While in Iraq, I met Dr. Chantay White, a clinical social work/therapist, who worked for the US Embassy in Baghdad. She explained that when a victim can speak about the event without crying, they have healed. It does not mean the event is completely wiped from your memory. As feelings may resurface, it means the event no longer has control over you. You have found a new way of being in the world; you may never be the same as you were before, but you do not have to view yourself as less.

You can emerge with newfound insights with the right support, discovering inner strength and spirit you didn't know you possessed. You may find your actual purpose in this life, one that never crossed your mind before, one that will bring you more joy than you can imagine. You are no longer a Victim; you are not a Survivor; you are a _Thriver_. Evidence of this stage can be reflected in a healthy lifestyle, humble but assertive attitude and positive decision-making process outcomes. It is time to enjoy this life and find out what kind of person you are now.

With anything in life, people who have never been through what you are going through, faced with your life decisions, will never fully understand. So, do not let these people be an influence on you regarding this type of matter. Just "About Face and Move Out," set the boundary of support. If someone is not promoting your recovery, turn away from them. Now, let me clarify something here. This does not mean blow off your supervisor because you have decided to do the work in the recovery process and think it gives ground to not fulfill the duty or a mission at hand while screaming, "I am taking care of myself!" Counseling appointments can be scheduled after duty hours, especially if it is with the Vet Center. If not, work out a schedule that aligns with the supervisor's intent and overall mission. The supervisor should be involved in ensuring you have access to everything you need. Communication is the key. It is a must to be flexible in your recovery as it is a long process. If your supervisor does not know about the incident, then schedule appointments outside of the duty day, or if an appointment is with the OBGYN, that is sufficient to say and schedule during the duty day. The recovery process is a personal journey with support.

Remember that sexual assault does change you, it does not reduce you, and most certainly, it does not define you. You are not a Victim; you are not a Survivor; you are a THRIVER!

LOCUS OF CONTROL

Beverly D. Johnson, Major, Engineer, Army

I can be changed by what happens to me,
but I refuse to be reduced by it.

-Maya Angelou

When I was young, many of our friends became extended family. I referred to my mother's female friends as "Aunt" and their husbands as "Uncle." My mother liked to entertain, so we always had extended family at our home. This was wonderful as a little girl, but as I grew, these extended family relationships led to complications. I matured into a full-figured adult-looking woman by age 13. I was always tall, around five feet eight inches, which added to my mature look. One day, at an "extended family" social event, one of my uncles, whom I would normally give a peck-kiss when he arrived at the house, decided to get a full-mouth kiss and stick his tongue in my mouth. Although I had never kissed a boy, I knew his actions were wrong. After the party ended, I told my mother what happened. It has been almost 40 years since that incident. I don't know what my mother did or said to the man, but he was never welcome to my home again, and I never spoke with or saw him again. The actions my mother took to protect me, and to ensure that I knew what happened was not my fault, set a precedence for the rest of my life.

Later, during my education I learned about "Locus of Control," which is a concept developed by Julian B. Rotter in 1954. It has since become an aspect of personality psychology. Locus of Control examines how much control people believe they have over events that influence their lives. This concept helped me understand many of the things happening around me and how I chose to respond to them. Locus of Control is the degree to which an individual feels a sense of control in his or her life. Someone with an internal Locus of Control will believe that things happening to them are greatly influenced by their own abilities, actions, or mistakes. A person with an external Locus of Control will tend to feel that other forces, such as random chance, environmental factors, or the actions of others, are more responsible for the events that occur in their life. Locus of Control falls on a spectrum and genetic factors may influence one's Locus of Control, as well as an individual's childhood experiences, particularly the behaviors and attitudes modeled by their early caregivers. Research has suggested that those with an internal Locus of Control are more successful, healthier, and happier than those with a stronger external Locus. External Locus of Control is believing others control our destiny where internal Locus of Control states that we control our destiny.

Julian Rotter proved that most people process their events either internally or externally. There are two thoughts on the origin of how a person views their personal control over the events in their life. Some believe that we are born with Locus of Control, that it is an innate part of your personality. Others believe that parents play an important role in the development of Locus of Control. Either way, the outcome is how we process things in life and the way these experiences influence our thought process. Understanding Locus of Control can provide insight into the motivations and attitudes of ourself and others.

Locus of Control is most widely believed to be a learned trait, not a personality characteristic that one is born with. The good news is, if the results you are getting now in life are not what you want, then you can change them through reading, listening to audio books, attending seminars, webinars, and workshops. We do have the ability to effectively influence our own lives. On the flip side, there are still some things which are out of our control. We cannot control other people's actions, opinions, feelings, or mistakes. However, we *can* control our own attitudes, effort, behaviors, thoughts, and actions. Below is a guide to help identify your Locus of Control:

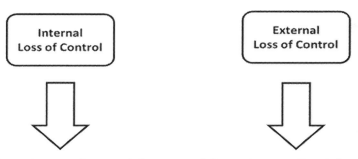

Internal Loss of Control	External Loss of Control

-Believes outcomes are in your control
-Experiences are shaped by your work and skill
-Do not seek the approval of others
-Take full responsibility for your actions
-You make things happen
-Less likely to conform to Social Influences

-Believes outcomes are the out of your control
-Seeks affirmation from others before action
-Experiences are the result of luck or chance
-Not confident in own skills, abilities, or knowledge
-Things happen to you
-More likely to conform to Social Influences

WHAT DOES ALL OF THIS HAVE TO DO WITH SEXUAL ASSAULT SURVIVORS?

Sexual assault is extremely disempowering. A person is sexually assaulted because – and only because – someone decides to sexually assault them. A survivor often feels helpless, and completely out of control over what happens to them. Someone with an external Locus of Control who has been sexually assaulted will feel that the world is a random and chaotic place, and bad things are liable to happen at any moment. If you are a survivor of sexual assault, and you find yourself turning inwards for an explanation, it's important to recognize that what you are doing is attempting to make meaning out of chaos. You are trying to find a way to feel grounded again and to protect yourself in the future. But here is the best thing you can do with your feelings of shame and thoughts of self-blame: share them with someone you trust. The best antidote to shame is empathy, and that is not something you can get from within yourself. Talk to someone – a friend, family member, or therapist – about what happened, and express your concern that you wonder whether you could have done anything differently. Talking to someone will help you feel more connected and less alone. The world slowly begins to feel like a friendly place where sometimes people are awful, instead of an awful place where people try to deceive you by acting friendly. And maybe, over time, you will find that you do not need to blame yourself anymore.

WHAT DOES RESEARCH TELL US?

There is a study designed to investigate the relationship between victimization history and Locus of Control and how Locus of Control can assist in predicting the adjustment of adult survivors of childhood sexual abuse. Results reveal that Locus of Control and victimization status combined can predict a women's symptom severity as well as other potential problems such as depression, anxiety, and hostility. Women with a severe abuse history who have an internal Locus of Control report somewhat lower levels of distress than other women. Women with severe abuse and an external Locus of Control report extremely elevated levels of distress which are higher than women in any other group

FINAL THOUGHTS

I was blessed to have a mother that protected and helped me understand what happened was not my fault. I don't recall what my mother said or did, but I remember thinking she was such a bad ass to protect me against a man that was trying to take advantage of me. I can imagine how that situation might have escalated into something worse if I had not told my mother and received her protection. As women, we should understand a few things:

- We have a responsibility to stand up for ourselves, our children and each other, it makes a difference.
- As survivors of sexual assault, we are not responsible for what happened to us.

- Our anticipation and reaction to situations can inhibit, deter, and protect us from future, possibly worse circumstances.
- If we are either genetically given the gift of internal Locus of Control, or if we were raised to embrace our independence and control over our lives, we will heal faster from our circumstances. If we have an external Locus of Control, we need to seek help to deal with the stressors of our circumstances and develop a sense of independence and control, so the negative things that happen do not control our future.

The quote by Maya Angelou at the start of this chapter resonates with me and can help channel our responsibility to ourselves and our future, "I can be changed by what happens to me, but I refuse to be reduced by it."

WALK IN RIGHTEOUSNESS TO JUSTICE

Nancy Griego, Colonel (R), Nurse, USAR

And this righteousness will bring peace.
Yes, it will bring quietness and confidence forever.

-Isaiah 32:16

I am an Army brat, born at Irwin Hospital, Fort Riley, Kansas, home of the Big Red One (BRO). My father completed his duty, and we moved to a small town in the Panhandle of Texas. I graduated High School, received my Associates Degree in Nursing from Amarillo College, Baccalaureate Degree in Nursing from West Texas A&M, and Master's Degree in Christian Ministries from Liberty University. I joined the US Army Reserve, Nurse Corps. retiring after thirty years of service in 2016. I received my Certification as a Sexual Assault Nurse Examiner and Legal Nurse Consultant. In 2017, I retired and would care for my elderly mother, so I decided to go back to school and used my GI Bill to complete a certification online in Culinary Arts and Pastry Arts. Now I bake and raise sheep. I do not know what else I want to do when I grow up.

At the age of twelve, I experienced my first suffering loss when my grandfather died. He had lived with us several months after his diagnosis of kidney failure. I recall waking to see my mother up many nights without sleep as she cared for him. He was proud of his American

Comanche Indian heritage and did not hesitate to tell everyone his grandkids were Indian. I remember kids on the school bus ridiculing me with Indian pow wow sounds and hoop dancing. He showed me how to drive, taught me how to be aware of my surroundings and watch out for boys. He had been a radio announcer, sheriff deputy and notary in our rural farm community. It seemed, everyone had high regard and respect for him. His wife, my grandmother, was also widely known around the Panhandle as the midwife. She delivered five of my seven siblings and most of the community. My grandparents would lay the foundation to my life and career.

My father of seven girls and one boy sent us to a Catholic school, taught us to speak without fear, listen frequently, and fight for what is right. He said we could become who we want if we went about it the right way. At the age of sixteen, I suffer a violation to my innocence. On the first day of my high school training job, I walked proudly to my first job. I was introduced to the company boss who led me to a chair and desk, where I would be working. He gave me an introduction to the job duties. I looked straight at his eyes with interest in all he said. He walked behind me to direct my view to a typewriter and that was when I began to feel uncomfortable. He began touching my shoulders and then reached to touch my thigh. I felt extremely uncomfortable, and knew it was wrong. I remembered my grandfather's advice as I looked at my surroundings toward the closest exit. I feared for what he would touch next and stood up from my chair abruptly. I did not tell him I was leaving and stormed out as quick as I could. He laughed with ridicule as I left. He had violated my space and the new job pride I had once felt was now gone. I did not want another job since this one had failed. I went home and told my father as I cried and felt shame. Both my parents told me it was the right thing to do, and I could always get another job. My father took care of the incident with the school and the company. The school cancelled that contract and the company later moved out of the community. I was convinced my parents could move mountains. My mother frequently told me not to trust boys if they got too close to me. I was not sure what that meant, but I was certain that an adult man touching me without my consent could not be trusted. My parents would be the foundation to my career and life.

I knew I wanted to be a nurse when I was in high school although my counselor indicated I would probably do better as a secretary. A US Army recruiter came to our high school, and I was curious if I could pass the entrance exam. I did not score well as a secretary however I did score well in the medical field. I graduated from high school, and at first did not go to college nor the Army. As most young teens, I rebelled and thought I could make my own decisions, so my adult life started with a marriage at the age of eighteen and my first child was born nine months later. I still recall a wedding memory of my father standing with me as we waited to walk down the aisle. The music started and he looked at me and said, "are you sure you want to do this?" I responded with a proud "Yes!" I was sure marrying a man eight years older than myself, who had already been married and divorced, was the right decision at the age of eighteen. The next ten years convinced me that an eighteen-year-old does not always make the right decisions and suffers consequences.

We had two wonderful children, a daughter and son. At the age of eight, my daughter suffered through a violating experience that she would keep to herself for many years. We had attended a conference at a convention center with close friends and stood around talking afterward. The children were running around and playing hide and go seek. They would run into elevators and go up and down the floors unbeknownst to the adults. One man, who was a dear friend, who would be the perpetrator, stepped into the elevator as my daughter waited to get to the next floor. He placed his arms against the wall as if to pin her underneath him and kissed her on the mouth. The elevator door opened, and she ran out quickly and never saw him again that day. This man was married and had a family. He was well respected and dear friend of ours. She never told us about this incident, although did tell her best friend, who also knew him.

Several years later, my daughter and I heard news reports of a local man who had impregnated two young twelve-year-old girls in our hometown. This was the same man who had violated my daughter as a child. I was shocked of the news and did not believe it until my daughter verified it with her experience. I was shocked by this man and felt horrible that my daughter never told me or her father. I asked her why she never told us about the incident, and she said she did not want her father to go to jail because he would most likely kill him. She felt bad for not telling us and had she told us, she may have prevented future incidents. My child feared for her father and she kept her distance from the perpetrator. She was relieved to know that he would no longer have that opportunity.

My husband and I divorced after ten years of marriage. Now my children would suffer the loss of a father at home and a mother who would now go to school, work two jobs, join the US Army Reserves and spend less time with them. I thank the Lord for my parents who always supported me as I completed my nursing degree and fulfilled my obligation to the Army. I began taking my children, now 13 and 8, with me to monthly Army drills and they enjoyed learning what I did.

In 1982 I completed my Nursing Degree and started my career in healthcare. I have a passion to this day, in caring for people. I took my nurses oath seriously; I swear by God Almighty to practice my profession with honesty, integrity, and faithfully. To devote myself to the welfare of those committed to my care. To develop myself and my profession. I started my career in a hospital emergency room as a Registered Nurse and experienced all types of emergencies. I saw all types of physical and psychological trauma, drug overdoses, medical emergencies, labor and deliveries and sexual assaults. This traumatic violation to women and children is what directed my passion to be a Sexual Assault Nurse Examiner and later a Legal Nurse Consultant.

In the mid-1990s, hospitals began Sexual Assault Nurse Examiner (SANE) programs for registered nurses. I was one of two nurses who attended the two-week course. It was the most graphic and interesting course I had taken throughout my medical career. We started our own SANE program at our hospital and began seeing patients. We had a 24-hour on-call rotation, and it seemed I was seeing most of them. I spent hours at the hospital and did not get much sleep for the first year, but other nurses took an interest and our schedule was easier.

My first victim was a five-year-old child brought in by her father and stepmother. They were concerned because the child frequently expelled flatus (gas) with most physical movements. This child had lived with her mother in another state for the past year and now was back with her father. The father informed me that his ex-wife was a drug addict, and they were divorced. He had remarried recently, and she had noticed the awkward noises the child made when she stood, ran or just moved when changing clothes. The stepmother and father questioned the child, but she did not reveal or know why she made the noises.

As a SANE nurse, I must be explicit and graphic when presenting a case to a jury. This case includes all the procedures used for forensic collections discussed later. I began my assessment with obtaining a history from her father and then asked if they were comfortable if I spoke to her alone. They agreed and remained outside the exam room door. To my surprise, the child did not express any fear or anxiety while alone with me. This was not a normal reaction for a five-year-old in a strange environment or with a stranger. I spent the next three hours with this child. I asked her questions about her home environment, her mother and others who may have lived or been in the home frequently. She informed me her mother was sick and had several men friends that gave her money to buy medicine. I asked her if they were nice men and if she like them. She said she frequently danced like a ballerina for them and they loved her. Those words led to more questions.

I asked if she would show me her ballerina dance. She proceeded to dance and as she jumped, darted, bent or turned I could hear a swishing of air or gas. I asked her where the noise came from and she revealed that it came from bottom. I then turn to questions about the men who loved her. She informed me that they gently touched her "gina," pointing to her genitalia, with their tongue and then their "willie." She mentioned their willie sometimes rubbed her too hard, but she could tell them to stop. She said sometimes they would put willie in her mouth and all she had to do was lick it like an ice cream cone. She revealed her mom allowed the men to love her with one stipulation, they could only touch and rub her mouth, anus and vagina.

I began the exam with her permission, which was not normal for a girl without the presence of a parent. I continued to question as I examined her from head to toe. She informed and showed me how these men would touch, kiss and lick her face, neck and most of her body. What they did with their tongue on her "gina" and "bottom," namely her anus.

She explicitly opened her legs to give me an open view of her genitalia and bend over to show me her anus. I was shocked to see her distorted vaginal labia (outer lips of vagina) and what might be a flat clitoris. This is caused by constant rubbing to the area preventing normal growth in a child. She literally bent over so I could see her anus. I could hear the swishing of air coming out of a 1-inch diameter opening of her anus. She obviously had been penetrated numerous times. She confessed that holding her "poop" was difficult. The physical exam exhibited other areas of this child's body that had been abused by perpetrators and the psychological abuse was just as traumatizing.

I referred this little girl to a child psychologist who could help reduce the risk of serious problems that the child will develop as an adult. The child's parents were given resources for family therapy to better help her. Law enforcement was notified as well as Child Protective Services. I prepared my case and presented it to a jury, and the perpetrators have been sentenced. This case would last almost two years, but the outcome prevented further abuse by these perpetrators.

This child had been trained and molded by these adults. Child sexual abuse is defined as any sexual act with a child performed by an adult. It includes sexual intercourse, sexually touching a child as well as non-touching offenses and sexual exploitation. This may include activities that do not necessarily include physical contact such as indecent exposure, showing the child pornography, and using the child to create pornography.

Childhood sexual abuse is a traumatic experience that has many consequences throughout the person's life. Victims are more than likely to experience higher levels of depression, guilt, shame, self-blame, eating disorders, anxiety, dissociative patterns, repression, denial, sexual and relationship problems. The rates of sexual assault prior to entering the military have been reported as 30% among women and 6% among men. (Sexual Assault in the Military; Curr Psychiatry Rep (2015)) Sadly, but the fact remains that being a victim puts one a much higher risk of being assaulted again. This is referred to as revictimization. One study concluded that being sexually assaulted once meant a woman was 32 times more likely that others to be revictimized. This makes it more challenging to combat sexual assault in the military if the leadership is unable to identify the most vulnerable within the ranks, hence the need for the *In Her Boots* program and the education and implementation of the services that a SANE provides.

I was deployed to Iraq in 2003-2004. We had just arrived in Kuwait and there was absolutely nothing that appeared to be a base. There were contractors setting up latrines, laundry facilities and dining halls. There were a few large tents with military personnel, but it was the beginning of what later would become the R&R for Soldiers. I remember the lack of latrines available. Males and females had to share latrines as well as so-called open barracks. As a female Major and leader, I informed our females not to go unaccompanied anywhere. We had to stay together and if a male was with them, they had to report where they were going and who the individuals were. Our Soldiers remained safe throughout our two weeks in Kuwait although at least four females were sexually assaulted in the latrines during the hours of 11pm and 12am and 5am to 6am. The perpetrator knew when these Soldiers were taking showers or going to or coming from work duties. The women reported their assaults, and the perpetrator was prosecuted. The combat zone did not stop this crime. The perpetrator knew some of the victims and others he did not.

While in Iraq the same year, I was summoned by my Commander to assist with a sexual assault crime. He knew I was a SANE, when previously questioned about the acronym on my bio. He offered my services at their morning meeting. The next day I was scheduled to meet a Captain, who was the investigator. I wondered if they would have a Rape Kit (former name of Sexual Assault Exam Kit) out in the combat zone and to my surprise, he did. Also, to my surprise, the Captain did not have any experience with Sexual Assault cases, nor did he know what a SANE was or what I did. I quickly educated him and questioned him about the victim. I wanted to examine her as soon as possible in order to get forensic evidence. He was not aware how he would use the Rape Kit, so I informed him I would be using it. I told him it was essential to maintain a chain of custody with the Rape Kit. His eyes lit up and he informed me, he could guard it with his life.

The victim was a young female Private who fell in love with a middle-aged married E6. She had been assigned to his detachment, and he convinced her he would divorce his wife if she gave herself to him. She stood her ground and wanted to see the divorce before she would give herself. She was a smart girl. He became frustrated that she wouldn't submit to him, so he took matters into his own hands. He sexually assaulted her, and she reported him to the Military Police. I told you she was smart.

It had been right at 72 hours when the incident happened, and she had bathed and changed her clothes. I obtained vaginal and anal samples, took all clothing she wore during the assault and samples from her hairbrush and bedding where the incident occurred. As she cried with embarrassment, she gave me a lengthy history with details. She apologized for crying, and I assured her it was ok to cry as much as she wanted. I documented as much information she could give. I took photos of bruises, bites and injuries she sustained. I thanked her for being patient with me since the process lasted about three hours and gave her my phone number to call me if the military judicial system missed or lost anything with her case. I assured her I could be at her trial if she needed me. I provided her with the limited resources I knew were on the FOB (Forward Operating Base) and recommended to her Commander that she be allowed to go home if she wished for recovery and victim assistance. I completed the Rape Kit and proceeded with the chain of custody process with the investigating Captain.

I returned to my duty location and later was relieved to hear she had returned home to be with family. The E6 was returned home facing criminal charges and discharge from the military. I was never summoned for a trial and never heard from this young Private. Justice was served.

Throughout my 10 years as a SANE, I examined; 10% adult males, 40% adult females and 50% children three months to 16 years old. My heart suffered with each case and sometimes I could not sleep thinking about these victims. I reminded myself frequently that justice would prevail.

As a Legal Nurse Consultant (LNC), I use expertise as a health care provider and specialized training to consult on medical-related legal cases, assist attorneys in reading medical records and understanding medical terminology and healthcare issues to achieve the best results for his clients. My role as an LNC only added to my expertise in court.

As a Sexual Assault Nurse Examiner, I provided compassionate care to aid the recovery of patients who are survivors of sexual assault. I collaborated and educated patients and their families to meet their health needs and aid in the recovery process. I utilized current evidence-based information and keep abreast of current trends in forensic and SANE nursing practices. I testified in court as an expert witness and assisted in preparing for court testimony. I collaborated with State Attorney's offices, Law Enforcement, Attorney General's Office and local victim services. I also worked closely within communities to educate on SANE programs and violence prevention.

The Sexual Assault Exam requires a private room, although I have obtained exams in the intensive care unit and surgery. Some facilities may also require a colposcopy, and camera for photographs. The procedure may take from 3-6 hours or in some cases longer. Every case is different and unique. Precise words, care, and documentation is a must. I have outlined, not in detail, the SANE exam to provide an understanding of the process.

The Forensic Medical Assessment starts with the Intake from Medical Personnel: any patient reporting acute sexual assault should be seen as soon as possible and triaged to assess for life- or limb-threatening injuries or psychiatric emergencies. These emergency injuries take precedence over forensic evidence collection. Once stable, a forensic medical assessment is offered. This assessment may take place before or concurrently with forensic sexual assault assessment, depending on facility policy.

The patient is escorted with family, caregiver or support person(s) and they are taken to a private waiting area. Safety is important. Is the suspect present? Speaking to the patient alone to obtain accurate information is important. I ask if there is any pain or bleeding and instruct patient not to use the restroom, change clothes, wash, smoke, eat or drink until evaluated by a forensic health care professional. If the patient must use the restroom, urine is collected. The victim is advised not to wipe genitalia until after evidence has been collected. The patient is referred to a sexual assault advocate for support and resource information. Then the Forensic health care professional is notified to begin exam.

The SANE is a Medical Forensic Examiner, although a SANE trained Nurse Practitioner and or trained Physician can perform the exam. Informed consent begins with the health care examiner introducing themself to the patient and describing the plan of care, their role, and expected time of completion. The patient can ask questions at any time. Patients can consent or decline any portion or all the forensic medical assessment. If the patient declines, they can return at another time. If they return within 120 hours since the incident, a Sexual Assault Exam Kit (SAEK) may be collected, however this delay may result in additional medical costs. The patient determines if they wish to report to law enforcement.

The medical assessment may take place before or concurrently with forensic sexual assault assessment. A verbatim history of the incident(s) is documented and includes those present during the patient's history and assessment. The time, date and location of assault(s) contact and/ or penetrative acts by suspect(s), any injury to suspect, if known, such as scratches, bites, punches, any use of lubricant, condom, saliva or objects, are documented. All patient actions between sexual assault and arrival to the facility such as brushing teeth, changing clothes, vomiting, using mouthwash or chewing gum, smoking vaping, swimming, douching, wiping genitals, and showering or bathing are noted. Questions will be asked such as; was patient menstruating at time of the assault or during the exam or wearing a menstrual cup or tampon? Did the suspect ejaculate and where? Was a weapon used or any physical force?

Evidence collection and packaging begins with a written consent or authorization prior to assessment and evidence collection. A mask and powder free gloves are worn by the forensic examiner when opening and inspecting the sealed Sexual Assault Exam Kit (SAEK). Gloves are changed often and between swab collections to prevent cross contamination. All clothing, including shoes, are inspected and collected to recover foreign matter for DNA or damage and placed into paper bags and sealed and only underwear goes in the SAEK. A prepackaged drug/substance-facilitated sexual assault (DFSA) specimen kit is used to collect urine and blood or if the patient experienced loss of consciousness, vomiting, nausea, dizziness that are unexplained by other causes. These specimens are sealed and labeled. Chain of custody is maintained for these specimens. All wet evidence such as swabs are air-dried prior to packaging and placed directly in swab boxes. Envelopes containing evidence are sealed with self-adhesive labels or tape. All evidence collected must have a time and date of collection and examiner's initials, patient name, date of birth, and a unique identifier number.

The swab and evidence collection process is explained to the patient before each site collection. Photographs per facility protocol are taken during the collection process. The purpose for collecting oral swabs around the mouth gum lines is to recover foreign DNA. These are collected when oral penetration or contact is suspected or patient experienced unconsciousness. A DNA buccal swab is obtained by swabbing the inner cheeks of the mouth and determines patient's DNA for comparison to other samples. A patient's clipped head and pubic hair is collected by cutting and combing through to collect trace evidence of foreign hairs. Any dry debris or secretions found are collected and swabbed. All body areas touched by the suspect are swabbed and collected for foreign DNA. The patient's fingernails are swabbed. Female patient's vulva, vagina, cervix, anus, or foreign retained object are swabbed. Male patient's penis, scrotum and anus are swabbed.

The documentation used is facility-approved forensic medical assessment forms. Facility protocol is followed for electronic or written documentation. Documents have a unique identifier. Documentation includes patient's pertinent medical and surgical history, last menstrual period, pregnancies, and medications. A copy of the documents is provided to law enforcement and the original copy stays at facility.

Chain of custody must be maintained and documented throughout the entire patient assessment and evidence collection processes. Chain of custody documents include the dates and times of everyone who handles every piece of evidence, from the time of collection through legal proceedings. For the non-reporting method, labels will have only the unique identifier or per facility protocols. Chain of custody documentation includes receipts, storage, transfer of evidence, and date and time and signature of each transfer or possession.

After the exam, the patient is given the option to take medications to prevent pregnancy and treat sexually transmitted diseases. She is given resources such as Crime Victim Center that provides Advocacy, counseling and legal assistance. The Victim's Compensation Program from The Office of the Attorney that can make payments and/or reimbursements to victims or claimants for eligible costs associated with the crime. Another resource for the victim is the Sexual Assault Victims Advocacy Center. The purpose for this center is to facilitate healing for victims and their families through on-going crisis intervention services.

I have learned that suffering is something which every human being faces. While no one likes to suffer, suffering does indeed bring about several positive benefits. One of the main benefits of my suffering was turning to God. Sometimes I was embarrassed to ask God for help but have learned to trust Him to develop my character. Suffering can help me reach out to others. When I see someone in a difficult situation it can cause me to reach out to that person and help his or her predicament. If I had not suffered, there would be no need to turn to God or others. Suffering makes me aware of my need for God and reminds me of his concern for me.

As a Soldier I stood and fought for our country. As a SANE I stood and fought for the victim and justice.

FROM THE HEART
Lisa Bass, Major (R), Engineer, Army

As senior female military leaders open the doors for the next generation, I believe it is our inherent responsibility to show them how to go through those doors.

-Lisa Bass

I hope that you found something from this book to put in your tool kit, to use in the future to set you up for success from our shared experiences and wisdom. The proposed strategies are not just for sexual assault and harassment prevention, but to developed battle drills to be executed in your overall decision-making process for life. It is one thing to receive *information*, it is another to *understand* it, but when you fully grasp the *revelation* of it all then you can grow and become what you were created to be in this life.

I loved my journey in the military. It taught me skills to succeed on the battlefield. I have seen the good, the bad, and the ugly, but I never once regretted raising my right hand to serve my country. Life is a battlefield, and there are life skills that need to be learned in order to engage the unsuspecting enemy you will encounter. Currently, the tactical training for life is not a focus while on active duty, because the focus is on Uncle Sam's mission. We each have a personal mission; the military is just a chapter in our life. The beauty of it all, is that one chapter can set you up for success in all of your endeavors with the right perspective. You can learn how to use it to your advantage. That is the premise for the *In Her Boots* program, to show you how to succeed in the military and beyond. To posture female service members into becoming a woman veteran, who is proud of her service, joyful about life, and prepared to lead the way in the civilian world.

There is a saying, "when you're a kid, you don't realize you're also watching your parents grow up." The same holds true within the military ranks; at each rank achieved, the service member is still developing. We expect our leaders to know more than we do serving under them. This much is true, however the life skills development is lacking compared to the tactical skills sets military leaders are proficient in. This is an injustice to the growth of subordinates.

The *In Her Boots* program is my passion. I have studied the gaps in our training for overall success and, in collaboration with other senior military leaders, created a way to fill those gaps. We are the generation that has lived enough life both through the military and as veterans to provide guidance and advice to reduce the learning curve.

I am so grateful for these contributing authors, most of them who have been with me from the conception of TF SASA. If there is one take away from what we have shared, is that it did not matter where we start out at, in the end we arrived at the same conclusions about this journey in life and the skills it takes to navigate successfully.

We care about our sisters-in-Arms and want to assist their success both in and out of the military. We personally know the challenges. We have been *In Her Boots*!

ABOUT THE
IN HER BOOTS
PROGRAM

SOLUTIONS WITHIN THE RANKS

Janice Lembke Dombi, Colonel (R), Engineer, Army

I'm a very strong believer in listening and learning from others.

-Ruth Bader Ginsburg

LIFE SKILLS

To be your best, most confident self, you may need to learn life skills that are often not taught at home. Our military volunteers are a slice of the nation, and many of them are not learning essential life skills before they enter the service. Researchers make it their life's work to figure out why families do not instill life lessons and values at home. Numerous articles on the internet describe the absence of families teaching life skills and call on schools to teach the missing subjects. Families are calling on schools to teach everything from doing laundry to communicating in a hostile discussion. I cannot pretend to know everything that is broken in society that, if fixed, would improve our culture, but I can provide a few examples, and then you can examine your upbringing and that of your peers to identify gaps.

Screen time is just a start to the list of activities that detract from parents teaching life lessons to children. Parents (or in thirty-two percent of US homes, a single parent), get home from work and shopping to find the kids deeply involved in social media, eating in front of the television. Too tired to confront a situation, everyone is left alone in peace. There is not a discussion about the dangers of sending a nude photograph on the internet. There is not a discussion about setting boundaries when your boyfriend keeps asking you for the picture. Sexting, friends with benefits, and hooking up are probably not discussed and certainly not addressed with an environment's added intricacies of a 10 to 1 ratio of men to women. This is an example of what I mean by "life skills." These are specific skills you can learn and practice to be confident and influence what happens to you, skills that will provide tremendous power and give you tools to control and reduce stress in your life. You can learn and practice skills today, not just in a life-changing situation. There are skills that develop your confidence to maneuver in a male-dominant profession. Examples of these skills are setting and enforcing boundaries and communicating when you do not like being pressured into doing something you are not ready to do.

How do I know some people lack these skills? Women give me examples all the time. Several have told me they do not mind when men and women use sexually explicit vulgar language around them and even when used directly at them. One young Marine proudly said that she did not cry when groped by her unit members. Some women share that they were sexually harassed but did not do anything because it was not worth the effort. One-third of sexual assault cases started as sexual harassment. It is worth the effort to learn skills, so you have choices and the confidence to implement your decisions.

A young woman told me a male Soldier continued to come to her work area and sit on her desk with his legs spread open, preventing her from pulling her chair up to her computer without sitting between his legs. He asked her out several times, and she told him, "no." I asked her how she told him. The Soldier replied that she smiled and laughed a little because she did not want him to think she was mean. You are not being mean when you enforce a boundary. You are confidently stating your expectations. In a matter of minutes, this Soldier learned the intricacies of delivering a message. I sent her away with homework to establish the boundary with her unwanted visitor. At our next mentoring session, she reported that she firmly gave her message, and he had not been back. She was so proud of herself. She said she felt like she found a magic wand. She found a life skill.

There are many ways to enforce a boundary. Your level of assertiveness may change depending on the offender's reaction. Your message and delivery must be firm and clear. You may enforce a boundary in many ways, including leaving the room, talking to the offender, and getting help from a third party. You need to find your voice before it is an emergency, and you doubt yourself. The offender has total confidence that you will not be loud, and you will not cause a scene. You need to prove him wrong. Accepting or putting up with inappropriate behavior does not make you one of the guys nor will it make you a valued teammate. It makes your life more stressful and reinforces the military rape culture that has plagued women in the military for over 40 years. It is an individual responsibility to add life skills tools to your kit.

Many women put up protective shields to survive and thrive in the military. Some women admit putting up shields, some do not. Women voice one of the protective shields when she says she is "just one of the guys." Women can never be one of the guys; she can be one of the Engineers, one of the Officers, one of the squads, one of the personnel specialists, but never one of the guys. Protective shields may give a false sense of safety and cloud situational awareness. Remember from your earlier chapter, *Finding Your Voice*, confidence is situational. Maintaining the protective shield may influence women not to report a sexual assault or sexual harassment because it jeopardizes their mental picture of being one of the guys.

Unwanted sexual contact is not a problem unique to the military. US colleges and universities also report high rates of sexual assault among their student population. Extensive literature indicates that corporate America and Hollywood struggle to eliminate sexual assault and sexual harassment as well. The wide-spread occurrence of sexual assault and sexual harassment suggests it is, in fact, a national problem. In both the military and colleges, most victims and the assailants are in the 17-24-year age group. According to the Department of Defense's *Report to Congress on Sexual Assault in the Military*, 85 percent of victims know their attackers, with over half being their peers. These are teammates with whom we work, play video games, and go to clubs. Most attackers are not strangers jumping out of bushes as depicted on television and movies. Sixty-two percent of sexual assaults involve alcohol. An operations plan looks at "what if" scenarios. It would help if you took time to rehearse different scenarios in your mind, so you are not blindsided and so surprised you literally cannot find your voice. It would help if you did not have to worry about teammates and drinking too much alcohol. Society should teach life skills that reinforce dignity and respectful treatment for everyone. This education clearly is not happening. As women, we can choose to sit on the sidelines and wait for the culture to change or look for ways to use life skills to reduce your learning curve and put you ahead of the 17-24-year-old group.

No matter your age, be proactive, and assess your situation, just as you would look both ways before crossing a road. Chances are a car will not hit you, but you look both ways anyway. While the 17-24-year-old age group has the highest occurrence of sexual assaults, 65% of the assaults are divided among all other age groups. Practice using all your resources to achieve a high standard of being treated with dignity and respect. Where can you make the most significant impact? Use your skills of deduction. As an example, your team is sitting around waiting for formation. A few men pass around a cell phone with photos that make you uncomfortable and support the rape culture. You learned about different activities that support rape culture in your training.

A strong move is to get a male peer to bring up your concern. In this technique, you can tell your male peer the specific behavior that crossed your boundary. He can call out teammates for showing sexually explicit photos to each other. If you brought it up, the comment might not be as well-received as it is from a male. This technique is a strategic approach where you can use your voice through someone else. It has the added benefit of reinforcing to your peer what poor behavior looks like, and perhaps he will intervene without your prompting in the future. Should the men need to be told, showing the pictures to each other was inappropriate behavior? No, they should know that already because they too attended SHARP classes... but remember, we are not waiting and hoping for change. We are not silently sitting by waiting while teammates denigrate the value of women in their unit. With this action, you reduced your learning curve beyond your years. You found your voice and used your resources.

A skill that needs constant refinement is the ability to know the difference between healthy acclimation and groupthink. A simplified explanation of groupthink is when everyone goes along with an idea or behavior without independently evaluating the options. The need to belong to a unified team is more important than causing dissent and risking being ostracized by the group. Groupthink happens at the local unit level and the organization level. The 1991 Tailhook scandal resulted in leaders calling for culture change in the military. The subsequent 2017 Marines United scandal and numerous spin-off pornographic and rape promoting web sites illustrate that dangerous groupthink still exists.

Sometimes you can be so acclimated in culture; the military, a fraternity, or a sorority, for example, you do not even recognize the situation is caustic, should be any other way, or is dangerous. Without developing the skill to evaluate the difference between healthy acclimation and groupthink, it leaves you open to gaslighting. Gaslighting is a type of manipulation where someone, or a group, gets you to second guess what you know to be true. The gaslighter is someone you care about or whose opinion matters to you. The gaslighter may tell you that you are too sensitive or making a big deal out of nothing. They will deny they made a comment that you clearly remember. This behavior will persist until you are questioning yourself. You start to accept their poor behavior and become confused. You will find you are always apologizing and eventually stop standing up for yourself. Bottom line, you will have more anxiety and be less confident than you used to be, you will open yourself to being culled from the herd by a predator.

In the story of a 19th century science experiment, researchers found when they put a frog in a pan of boiling water, the frog quickly jumped out. On the other hand, when they put a frog in cold water and slowly turn up the heat, the frog adjusted. When the water boils over time, the frog just boiled to death. The hypothesis is that when the temperature change is gradual, the frog does not realize it is boiling to death.

While the story is probably an urban myth, the story's moral is a good metaphor for organizational culture. It recognizes that we need to teach life skills to gauge the temperature of the water.

SENIOR MILITARY WOMEN MENTORS

Every woman needs a senior female mentor, preferably not in her chain of command, where she can turn for training, advice, guidance, and support. Statistically, a woman will not have another woman in her Chain of Command. Ideal female mentors will have at least 15 years of service and be senior ranking in their military occupational skill. I recommend the senior woman not be in your Chain of Command for two reasons. If you are having a problem with a senior leader in your Chain of Command, and the offender is also in your unit, it might be the mentor's leader or possibly a peer, creating a conflict of interest. This existing relationship could, perhaps, influence the advice she provides. The second reason to have a senior female mentor outside your Chain of Command is to encourage candid discussion with you about the dangerous or foolish things she did as a young Servicemember. She will not be as concerned with who knows these personal details and may discuss better ways to proceed. I know this was my case when talking to subordinates. I found people from other units were less judgmental and more willing to hear the message or teaching point instead of focusing on my twenty-two-year-old self's regrettable behavior.

The first thing most senior leaders and Veterans say when they hear about a skill development program for a gender-integrated service is, "that's a leadership issue!" They follow with, "back in my day, the leaders took care of that." Actually, no one took care of it, and we know that because the culture did not change. I hear the same story repeatedly from women Veterans from the 1960s until our present day. When they reported a sexual assault, leadership told them to forget about it and encouraged the victim not to harm the promising young man's career. Back to my original point: teaching life skills, if not learned at home, must be a leader's responsibility.

There are very few servicemembers on active duty or the reserve components today who served before women were integrated into the military. Nearly everyone serving today is post-Navy WAVES, Army WACS, Air Force WAFS, and Coast Guard SPARS. Why aren't the currently serving leaders operating in an enlightened manner while leading today's servicemembers? Many of the current leaders and most of the junior leaders never learned and practiced the skills themselves, and they do not even know it. Since the war in Iraq started in 2003, and then the simultaneous war in Afghanistan, the military began a revolving door of deployments. Military units would serve in the war zone, return home to block leave, where everyone was on vacation simultaneously, reestablish family-life routines, re-set with equipment, and begin training for the next deployment.

In part because of deployments and accelerated promotions to meet the military's needs, Noncommissioned Officers (NCO) might have substantial combat experience but not life skills or subordinate development experience. The Noncommissioned Officer education system schools (NCOES), for professional development, could not keep up with the deployment cycle demands. As a result, fewer NCOs went to leader development school, and those that attended went years later at the next higher rank. The Rand Corporation completed a study that evaluated the value of experience in the enlisted force. They concluded that approximately 22 years of experience for an E-6 was the most beneficial for leadership development judged by the subordinate attrition rate, subordinate promotion rate, and subordinate demotion rate. The Rand study also highlighted that the top expectation Soldiers had for their NCOs was "taking care of Soldiers." On page 78 of the Rand study, the researchers concluded, "only [the Course for E-6 NCOs SIC] have had a major focus on leadership skills, and, even in this course, only a small amount of time is devoted to teaching NCOs the skills that directly relate to developing their subordinates. The percentage of time in other NCOES courses directly related to the development of subordinates' skills is much smaller and, for some courses during the period, was almost nonexistent."[1]

[1] Jennie W. Wenger, Caolionn O'Connell, Louay Constant, Andrew J. Lohn, Rand Corporation, *The Value of Experience in the Enlisted Force*, 2018, https://www.rand.org/pubs/research_reports/RR2211.html.

The NCOs and the junior Commissioned Officers, that the Platoon Sergeants also help develop, were doing the nation's important business fighting the wars and keeping subordinates alive. My point is, while they were keeping people alive, they were not conducting developmental counseling and modeling proper interpersonal skills and garrison behavior to subordinates. Unfortunately, to some people, the subordinate development tasks of interpersonal life skills are viewed as garrison duties and not rated as necessary in a war environment.

To further highlight a need for formal life skills training, the Army and the Marine Corps list the average time in service for E-7 at approximately 12.5 years. The Army promotion regulation lists the minimum time in service for promotion to an E-7 is six years. In my research, I could not find NCOs that achieved that goal in the Army, but the Navy had Sailors make E-7 in 5.5 years. I did find that many Soldiers and Sailors reached the more widely known "7 in 7." This term means promotion to the grade of E-7 in 7 years. So, in the Army's case, the senior leader, in an organization of approximately thirty Soldiers, was about 25 years old. These Senior leaders are only a few years older and, therefore, not much more experienced in interpersonal development than the charges they lead and mentor.

I will illustrate the insufficiency of maturity in some of the NCO corps in my next example. One evening in Iraq, women Soldiers were walking to the bathroom in their housing area. They were wearing lingerie tops and Army physical training shorts. A female Major stopped the women and directed them to return to their containerized housing unit (CHU) and get in proper uniform, which would add a T-shirt and reflective belt. When the soldiers left to comply, the Major asked the male NCOs in the area why they had not made an on-the-spot uniform correction? One NCO said he did not correct the women because he did not want a sexual harassment charge against him. Yes, this is a leadership issue. Leaders need tools and role models to act appropriately and learn techniques when something out of the normal presents itself. I am making a big assumption that these men would correct a male Soldier if he were out of uniform. If not, the men's homework assignment after the first formal training session will be extensive. These NCOs need formal training from senior mentors already in the service. The senior female mentors can assist the male mentors as well. The military already has the resources to make a change within the ranks.

Mentors are not there to circumvent your Chain of Command but help you use the Chain of Command to reach an agreeable solution. For example, in Iraq a Sergeant came to me and said a senior Sergeant was sexually harassing her. She reported the harassment, and the Commander decided to relocate her to another unit. She told me she did not want to move out of the company because she did not know anyone at the new location. I asked if she talked to her Commander, a Colonel, about the move. She said no, she was too nervous about speaking to him. I recommended she get a friend to accompany her to use the Commander's open-door policy and tell him how she felt. She liked that idea and said she did not know she could bring a friend with her. Two weeks later, I asked the Sergeant if she talked to her Commander. She said she had and that the Commander said he did not know she didn't want to move. He thought he was helping her, so she didn't have to see the senior Sergeant. The Commander reversed his decision on the relocation. She added that when other women in the unit saw she did not have to move after filing a complaint, three more came forward with information about the same harassing Sergeant. The Commander initiated an expanded investigation.

A senior female mentor can teach life skills she learned at the school of hard knocks. Because no similar program to *In Her Boots* existed to help her reduce the learning curve, she found out most lessons the hard way. The mentor can also help you fine-tune your radar to disrespectful or career influencing behavior that you have lived with every day and chalk it up as "the way it's always been done." I have been in two units where I was the only junior enlisted woman. The company leadership just assumed I would be the clerk-typist. It did not matter what my skill identifier was or that I could not type well. I was sent to the office to type because I was a woman. How do I know? The First Sergeant told me.

Years later, as a Battalion Commander, I saw many females sent to unit headquarters to be training clerks or other administrative clerks, keeping track of records. This was not an official job but adhoc as the work had to be accomplished by someone. In almost all cases, supervisors sent women to do the job. Since I was tuned in to being relegated to the office, I would ask the bulldozer operators and other engineer Soldiers how long they worked in the office. Many responded they were serving in the capacity for over a year. While they were filing physical fitness cards and marksmanship records, their peers were getting stick time out on the project sites and using the latest laser-guided equipment preparing for deployment. The women were all excellent Soldiers and would not have remained in the headquarters otherwise. A special detail is an exceptional experience to see how a headquarters functions and to learn regulations. However, this experience should be brief and spread out among both men and women, not to disadvantage anyone from developing technical skills and leadership abilities they will certainly need at the next rank. When these women return to the line and do not perform at their peers' proficiency level, it may cause friction and even delayed promotion because they were not technically and tactically proficient. As a senior military woman that walked *In Her Boots*, I could see the extended temporary assignment through a different lens. A woman mentor can do the same for you.

Another area a senior military woman mentor may assist is moving a complaint up the Chain of Command. A junior woman shared that she was at her work location in the motor pool when a male peer wrapped up a T-shirt and held it around his waist, simulating a penis. He preceded to jump around while poking her with the T-shirt penis. The onlookers laughed harder as she tried to swat him away with her hands. Later on, a friend showed her a cell phone video of the incident so she could take it to their supervisor. When the Soldier showed the video to her Noncommissioned Officer supervisor, he laughed. The complaint went no further. The woman responded that she was demoralized, and her duty performance began to slip. She reported that she was facing non-judicial punishment. Instead of setting the right example, her supervisor reinforced the current military culture. I can think of several ways a senior woman mentor could have stepped in and helped the young woman find firm footing to go to the next person in her Chain of Command.

Here is one final example where a senior woman mentor could have made a world of difference: I talked to a Veteran at an insurance conference, and she told me she enjoyed the military but got out as soon as she could. She said her Commander said she would never get promoted unless she slept with him. If this junior officer were my mentee, I would first pull out the regulation to show her in black and white how the promotion system works. Then I would accompany her, unannounced, to visit the Commander during his open-door hours. After we both sat down, I would tell the Commander that I heard he had an interesting promotion policy and ask him to explain it again. Having the mentor involved lets the predator know his behavior is no longer a secret, and the mentor would be monitoring for retaliation against the woman for reporting this sexual harassment.

The high number of sexual assaults in the US Military indicates that the culture must change to reflect a society where men and women are treated with dignity and respect. Military and Civil leaders have repeatedly called for culture change, and women have waited for this promised change since the Navy disbanded the WAVES in 1948. Instead of waiting for the culture to change, women service members need to take action and improve their confidence, including confidence with sexuality, to set and enforce boundaries. For culture change to occur, both men and women need to learn life skills taught by senior military leaders. The senior military women have an inherent responsibility to help transform the culture and remain an untapped and vital resource already in the ranks.

IN HER BOOTS IS A COMMANDER'S PROGRAM

Janice Lembke Dombi, Colonel (R), Engineer, Army

Insanity is doing the same thing over and over again and expecting different results.

-Unknown

IN HER BOOTS IS A COMMANDER'S PROGRAM

Ultimately it is a program to take care of all servicemembers and improve unit readiness. Our goal is to use the wisdom and experience of senior military women who served *In Her Boots*, integrated with programs the military has already invested in our servicemembers. The *In Her Boots* program is about educating, empowering, and inspiring women to increase their confidence level. With greater confidence, the occurrence of sexual assaults and sexual harassment will go down as women stand up for themselves and call out sexual harassers and predators. Their behavior will reinforce "Prevention before Reaction." The *In Her Boots Program* is a refreshing new approach to changing values and decision making. It is not "the way we've always done it" because our past efforts involve single classes promoting the redundant information taught by leaders with the knowledge that is Powerpoint-slide deep. The more recently added "By-stander Intervention" is also a presentation. Changing the culture of the military will take more than slides and much more than skits. It will take prolonged work with an educational program involving small group hands-on training for participants. *In Her Boots* supplements the existing plan that uses programs already deployed by the military in Sexual Harassment/Assault Response and Prevention (SHARP), the military legal system, and the medical system. All of these current programs are skewed heavily toward *response* after a sexual assault. *In Her Boots* is loading the program on the front end for *prevention*.

The Department of Veteran Affairs estimates 20-25 percent of servicewomen are sexually assaulted. This statistic leaves 75-80 percent of women that predators did not attack. What are the skills and tactics that servicemembers can learn to make more predators turn away? *In Her Boots* provides the platform for information exchange and problem-solving to take place. The classes are facilitated by senior military women mentors, preferably not in the servicemember's Chain of Command, who can help when a developing situation is beyond their control. These mentors can also provide advice if a woman needs guidance in approaching the Chain of Command. Based on our experience, the senior military women mentors need the training to take on this formal life skill development role since most women have not had a female mentor either. The *In Her Boots* program provides the mentors with assistance through our facilitator manual. Developing confidence and mentoring women is the *In Her Boots* program.

I anticipate a concern that senior leaders reading this chapter will have. Your schedule is already packed. I agree. I was in your boots too. I commanded two Engineer Combat Battalions (Heavy), a Brigade level command, and a Division in the US Army Corps of Engineers (USACE). I wish I had this program as a Battalion Commander. The week I took command, I had six women come to my open-door policy and tell me about sexual harassment and sexual harassment retaliation from the previous six months. The time spent with investigations, including interviews, talks with leadership, and policy and system reviews, far exceeded the time it would have been to meet with a few women for an hour each month. Over the following months, I was conducting brown bag lunch sensing sessions anyway, so one session could have been the mentoring meeting. It is heartbreaking when women trust senior leaders to investigate an alleged attack, and the leader cannot find supporting evidence. Not *won't* find evidence, *can't* find proof. The accused has a right to an evidence-based charge as well. Opening lines of communication and helping women determine their sexual values and establish and enforce boundaries will help women take control of their sexuality and give well-intentioned men, that want to do what is right, the opportunity. On the other hand, some predators are just as violent, conniving and ill-willed as any enemy we face on the battlefield. Power and control are his lifeblood. He is looking for the gazelle to cull from the herd. Giving the women tools to navigate out of a dangerous situation, a will to escape, and the courage to make a colossal scene in the process can be empowering as well.

We cannot continue to curse the system, wring our hands, and wait for culture change. Civil and military leaders have promised military culture change for years. Many people thought things will finally change with the elimination of the US Coast Guard Women's Reserve (SPARS) in 1973, Women's Air Force (WAF) in 1976, and the Women's Army Corps (WACs) in 1978. Women were again hopeful for a catalyst for culture change after the lid blew off the 1991 Tailhook scandal in Las Vegas, revealing the vile cancer in the ranks from the most senior leaders down. We were promised culture change after numerous scandals at basic training posts, including drill sergeant and training instructor sex scandals at Aberdeen Proving Ground, Maryland, Fort Leonard Wood, Missouri, and Lackland Airforce Base, Texas. Headlines put a spotlight on sexual assaults at the US Military Academies. The award-winning 2012 documentary, "The Invisible War," enraged the public and Congress. Many military women thought surely, the culture will change now. Who can watch this film and not see how screwed up the culture is? The *Military Times* even published a 2018 article, "Sexual Assault: Here are the bases where troops are most at risk."[2] The recent

---

[2] Tara Copp, *Military Times*, "Sexual assault: Here are the bases where troops are most at risk," Sept 21, 2018, https://www.militarytimes.com/news/your-military/2018/09/21/sexual-assault-here-are-the-bases-where-troops-are-most-at-risk/

2020 in-depth investigation and subsequent 136-page report by the independent review committee at Fort Hood, Texas, echoed the need for a culture change.[3] The lack of substantial progress in changing the military culture is not only noted by women in uniform. According to House Armed Services Personnel Subcommittee Chairwoman Jackie Speier (D-Calif.), "little has changed in 40 years, except we have thrown a lot of money at this problem." I estimate it is close to a billion dollars now. What do we have to show for it? I have spent 10 years on this issue. I do not take any pride on the numbers going down or going up because, frankly, for all that we have done not much has changed.[4] The military needs to stop doing business as usual and expecting a different outcome. It is easy to have a unit fun run, bake sale, march in women's high heels, and smash a vehicle with a sledgehammer to show support for sexual assault awareness month. Men and women both need to roll up their sleeves and put in weekly work and monthly structured lessons to make a significant and lasting change.

Civil and military leaders will need to enforce programs, regulations, and laws to change the military's culture. Like any good obstacle plan, you need to have a defense in depth covered by fire. The United States' national culture and laws are defenses beyond the horizon. Military culture gets closer to you as people from the United States, and the varied cultures of the 35,000 non-U.S. citizens that serve in the US military, join the ranks. Regulations and firm policies are in this layer of defense. Local Sexual Harassment and Sexual Assault Response Programs (SHARP), unit climate, and by-stander intervention actions attempt to stop the enemy from closing in. Suppose the obstacles in this defense plan fail as they have for thousands of servicemembers each year. We need to reduce the learning curve so you can find your voice. You need to be ready, with weapons in your kit and an operations plan in your back pocket, to recognize and appropriately act when someone crosses your boundary.

---

[3]   The Report of the Fort Hood Independent Review Committee https://www.army.mil/e2/downloads/rv7/forthoodreview/2020-12-03_FHIRC_report_redacted.pdf accessed 15 Dec 2020.

[4]   Scott Maucione, *Federal News Network, Army says junior leaders not handling sexual harassment correctly, July 29, 2020,* https://federalnewsnetwork.com/army/2020/07/army-says-junior-leaders-are-not-handling-sexual-harassment-and-assault-correctly/ accessed Dec 5, 2020.

Sexual assaults and sexual harassment happen in all age groups and to men as well as women. In the military, because of the large number of men, numerically, there are usually more sexual assaults against men than women. Attacks on men are generally by other men or groups of men and women. Because of the stigma involved with sexual assault, men often classify their assault as hazing or bullying. Proportionally, there are more assaults against military women each year, including a 38% increase between 2016 and 2018, according to DODs most recent survey. What makes the military unique compared to other populations is the significantly higher ratio of men to women and the importance of teamwork to accomplish a mission.

FORMAL STRUCTURED TRAINING

Task Force Sisterhood Against Sexual Assault (TF SASA) understands and fully supports the importance of having a gender-integrated team. With women's expanding role in combat arms, it is more important than ever that they can stand confidently with their team. Dividing up a team for training is not a new concept. Sometimes drills and training are tailored for the team's specific subcomponents. The funeral detail practices each component of the mission separately before executing as a team. The honor guard firing party practices their responsibilities separately from the flag detail. The bugler practices separately from the other two details. When each subsection is trained, then they join back together, they make a stronger high performing team. As dedicated teammates, everyone needs to execute their portion of the plan and operate the systems, whether they are personnel systems or weapons systems or machinery, with skill. Teamwork does not mean every minute of every day must be spent together in a group.

Women need a formal process to learn skills better to assist them with integration in the US military. We have already established the military is a male-dominant profession with a culture in significant need of change. The abhorrent sexual assault statistics indicate integration is not at the optimal level. As 15 percent of the military, women are a subcomponent that can benefit exponentially by training separately from the men when learning life skills. Women military leaders need to talk candidly and work a focused program with junior women to make a personal connection and encourage and enforce participation. The mid-grade leaders learn the skills and learn how to mentor so they can model confident behavior and eventually take over the training when they are the senior leaders. There are several skills that women can learn to improve their confidence and better represent themselves to subordinates, peers, and superiors alike. The most efficient and practical training to accomplish this task is single-gender training: high quality, small group separate training for women, training for men, and periodic SHARP training that would remain co-ed.

Some people will initially say this targeted skills training is not fair, and to that, I say, the fair is where you ride the Ferris wheel and eat corn dogs. I am not flippant; instead, I am looking at reality. You should be treated with dignity and respect all the time. You should be able to wear whatever you want; you should be able to drink alcohol and get drunk with whomever you want, and you should be able to socialize with whomever you want. That is a lot of "shoulds" to overcome. Living in today's culture, however, it is risky behavior not to evaluate your surroundings and make prudent decisions. If you insist on using the word "fair" to define necessary training, refocus your anger. The Department of Defenses' surveys from 2005-2019 report 34,000 – 20,500 military sexual assaults each year. Now that is not fair.

Some leaders may not want to separate the women and men for training because they believe the women are getting together to bash men. The training core is to reinforce dignity and respect for everyone, so we recommend you always allow male leaders to come to the training as long as they remained in the background. In our case, after male leaders saw the high-quality training and extensive participation, they better understood the formal program's intent. When TF SASA brought the development program to units, we would always pre-brief the Command and senior NCOs. Without exception, the first reaction was to push back and reject the training. When we further explained to the leaders that we talk to the women about consenting to sex or verbally not consenting to sex to eliminate many he-said/ she-said (or more frequent, he-did not say/she-did not say, situations), they saw benefits to the unit and readiness and supported the training.

Many military women, both junior and senior, do not believe there is a need for female mentors. This might be you right now. Women have been programmed for so long to think that there is no difference between women and men that there will be resistance to a life skills program, especially one that separates men and women. After 121 reported sexual assaults in a matter of months, the Army's III Corps Command Sergeant Major permitted TF SASA to conduct training during deployment. Our initial one-day "Finding Your Voice" conferences were mandatory for women. With arms crossed against their chests and hunched down in their seats, the women admitted they were "voluntold" to attend. They said past "women's only" training centered around wearing makeup while in uniform, hair standards, shopping, and other casual activities for which they had no interest in spending time. Without exception, and without prompting, women in the audience always revealed personal stories that they had never told anyone before. They felt safe to share after seeing the senior leader presenters' venerability. After each conference, the local mental health provider told us she saw a spike in clients as women came forward to begin their sexual assault recovery. The two-way sharing opens women to consider alternative approaches and encourages them to reduce risky behavior. The sharing builds trust in leaders, so they begin work on skills to develop their voice. By the end of the day, women are not saying they were voluntold to attend but were asking how they can get more. The high-quality women-only experience also made them receptive to the idea that things can improve in their circumstances once they find their voice.

Others may reject being a mentor or needing a mentor because they have been "doing just fine" without one for their entire career. A whole career can be anywhere from 1 and 30 years. "Fine" does not represent the standard of our military. "Fine" does not represent the thousands of women sexually assaulted each year, and Veteran's Administration Military Sexual Trauma clients, and unfortunately, suicides related to sexual assault in our military.

Finally, the training needs to be women-only because, frankly, women will not candidly talk if men are present. The fact remains, men and women communicate differently achieving the same end state. There are scores of current scholarly studies discussing the American education system and the flawed role in developing confident women.[5] This is a controversial issue, and I recommend you research this on your own. Girls learn to raise their hands to speak at an early age while boys take matters into their own hands to get the attention and time with the teacher. When girls and boys answer questions, boys get more praise, and girls receive more corrections. This unintended discrimination continues to shape women today despite teachers' efforts to treat children fairly. A recent survey by Gallup found that women are less likely to speak up in the classroom if their opinion differs from their male peers.[6] Women speak less in college seminars and frequently apologize while giving their answers or comments. The author of the article "Women speak up less in college seminars—here's why that matters, the author discusses the importance of answering questions and discussing topics without continually apologizing. Separate gender training will allow women to practice the necessary skills without competing for time with male peers.[7] Every SHARP class I taught or attended eventually turned into a shouting match over gender-specific standards of the physical readiness test and accusations of false claims of sexual assault. Women will be able to talk to each other about the topic for the day and not have to defend issues for which they have no control.

Women participating in the *In Her Boots* monthly skill training sessions told us the classes left them feeling energized and powerful as they returned to their units. Remember, not believing you have options adds stress and a feeling of victimization. Women left with plans to move forward in their minds and a tool to practice to gain confidence. Their pinpoint homework assignment was built around action and learning a skill.

---

[5] Kelvin Seifert and Rosemary Sutton, OER Service Educational Psychology Chapter 4, https://courses.lumenlearning.com/suny- Educational Psychology.:. Located at: https://open.umn.edu/opentextbooks/BookDetail.aspx?bookId=153. License: CC BY: Attributioneducationalpsychology/chapter/gender-differences-in-the-classroom/

[6] Jeremy Bauer-Wolf, " Speaking out in the Classroom" *Inside Higher ED,* June 3, 2019

https://www.insidehighered.com/news/2019/06/03/new-survey-shows-fewer-female-students-male-are-ease-sharing-uncomfortable-views accessed 12 Dec 2020.

[7] Kari Paul, "Women speak up less in college seminars—here's why that matters, " Market Watch, Published: Sept. 29, 2018 at 11:09 a.m. ET. https://www.marketwatch.com/story/women-speak-up-less-in-academic-settings-heres-why-that-matters-2018-09-28

The high number of sexual assaults in the US Military is an indicator that the culture must change to reflect a society where everyone is treated with dignity and respect. Military and Civil leaders have called for culture change, and women have waited for this promised change since the Navy disbanded the WAVES in 1948. Instead of waiting for the culture to change, women servicemembers need to take action and improve their confidence, including confidence with sexuality, to set and enforce boundaries. Both men and women need to learn life skills taught by senior military leaders.

In Her Boots is a Commander's program and uses the resources already in the military. The women-only training provided by women who have been *In Her Boots* will increase confidence and ultimately reduce the number of sexual assaults in the military. It is a formal program that requires self-improvement work, practice, and mentoring. This is not a one-shot-one-kill training approach. It is not a one-time skit, video game, or awareness training. We do not improve weapons marksmanship by watching a presentation. We have to get hands-on practice. A lasting culture change requires repetition of values and life skills, that we need to approach like any other military battle drill. The *In Her Boots* program can be the catalyst for how Commanders improve readiness and ultimately reduce sexual assault and sexual harassment in the military. We cannot wait any longer for culture change. We cannot solve the culture problem by having a near-peer flipping a stack of 150 PowerPoint slides. We need to roll up our sleeves and get to work.

IN HER BOOTS
Prevention *before* Reaction

In Her Boots is a different approach, creating a dialog between senior and junior female servicemembers that Educates, Empowers, & Inspires, targeting increased readiness, retention, and sexual assault prevention strategies.

Purpose:

- Task Force Sisterhood Against Sexual Assault (TF SASA) believes that improving confidence by developing life skills through education and camaraderie creates a positive change in attitude, behavior, and the decision-making process. This program is a different and lasting approach to preventing sexual assault and harassment. This program runs concurrently with "culture-changing" programs, which are taking too long to make the necessary changes to reduce sexual assaults in the military.
- TF SASA address issues head-on as senior military women speakers educate, empower, and inspire women by sharing personal experience with life lessons from their time in the service. Their stories frequently include experiencing sexual harassment and sexual assault themselves.
- TF SASA acknowledges the difference between the genders and communicates behaviors while targeting personal growth, emphasizing dignity and respect for everyone.

- TF SASA shares the "How To Do" versus "What To Do." This approach is different because it provides specific strategies for women to stand up for themselves as their first defense line.
- This program is open to all females. Topics are heavily weighted on communicating specifically to women. Senior male leaders' limited attendance and participation are encouraged as it allows them to hear firsthand the struggles and experiences from a female perspective.

Program Overview:

TF SASA is a different approach to the more common sexual assault training of "No means No,"; a message geared toward men, and bystander intervention, geared toward a third party. TF SASA focuses on teaching women to improve situation awareness and identify and enforce their boundaries.

- The program's general concept is a one day "Finding Your Voice" seminar, including senior military women from their base, followed by monthly workshops.
- Conduct a senior military women's workshop to explain the In Her Boots program and provide details and their crucial role in implementation.
- With various backgrounds and experiences, senior women become mentors for junior women. Senior Female service members drive this program for female service members allowing the mentees to make connections and communicate openly without fear of reprisal
- Monthly workbook assignments, provided by TF SASA, LLC, for the junior women's continued personal development and practice implementing the life skill taught at that month's workshop
- The Facilitator's guide, provided by TF SASA, LLC, is for mentors and parallels the mentee's workbook assignments. The guide significantly reduces the additional workload for senior military women to administer this program.

The Benefit to the Command:
READINESS AND IMPROVED COMMAND CLIMATE

- This program brings issues into the open in a non-hostile environment while providing education and confidence development. A sexual assault in a unit is exceptionally disruptive and often divides the entire organization into battlelines supporting one person or the other. Service members frequently believe the chain of command is at fault for prosecuting or not prosecuting the alleged offender—this discord and harms unit readiness. The *In Her Boots* Program provides women with confidence development tools to establish and enforce boundaries, significantly reducing the he said/she said harassment and support scenarios. Junior women also have a mentor to assist them with confronting inappropriate senior/ subordinate sexual harassment
- Women will no longer believe that "there was no one to tell" if they get in a threatening situation because they have a mentor that has walked "In Her Boots". The mentors can make recommendations for the women to enforce a boundary on their own. The mentors can help service members develop a plan to communicate problems to their chain of command if they cannot resolve an issue independently.
- In this forum, senior female leaders can gather information from the junior female service members to share trends with commanders. This program is another avenue for commanders to understand the command climate and a venue to develop trust with the service members.

HOW CAN WE PARTNER TOGETHER TO ELIMINATE MILITARY SEXUAL TRAUMA WITHIN OUR RANKS?

For More Information, visit
www.InHerBoots.org

Or Contact:

COL (R) Janice Lembke Dombi:
Janice@tfsasa.com

Or

MAJ (R) Lisa (Belcastro) Bass:
Lisa@tfsasa.com

DEDICATION

To my dear husband, Jerry Bass, who has stood beside me, encouraged me, and believed in me to finish this book that I started a decade ago; I am forever grateful for your faith in me.

After several years of being single, my grown children were encouraging me to start dating. I had been shelled shocked enough in that area of my life. At the same time, with everything I was doing that occupied my time, I was still alone. I had cherished my independence for many years, but I began to feel that something was missing. I did not have the first clue how to venture out in this area. Dating practices changed in the last couple of decades and my friends told me about this dating app, POF (Plenty of Fish). I pondered on that idea for another six months until one day I finally decided to give it try.

I felt my energy draining with each swipe of the pictures. Then I came across a man wearing a cowboy hat. I read his profile and saw he did not own any horses. Me, being passionate about horses, sent him a message in my true outspoken fashion and said, "What, cowboy hat and no horses?" I did not think any more about it. Weeks passed and I received a message that said, "I will have you know; I ran cattle when I was young and traded all that in for my 18-wheeler. I earned the right to wear my cowboy hat unlike those city boys in Dallas!" I immediate thought, *I like this guy, he might be able to keep up with me.* I agreed to meet him for Derby Day at the Grand Prairie, TX Horse Track. My daughter and I went shopping for a dress and a fancy hat like the ladies' wear for the Kentucky Derby; it was the first time we had fun since all the deaths.

I arrived at the place and knew who he was the minute I got out of my car at the valet parking. This man's face lit up like a light bulb. We enjoyed the races and conversation. When I got home, my daughter asked how it went and I said, "he will make a nice friend." We continued to go out, and immediately I began testing his character, as he did mine. That is one thing I admired about him. He had his boundaries.

I like to say, I cast out a line only once on *Plenty of Fish* and caught a Bass. I have been married to Mr. Bass for many years now. He tells me I make a good wife; I tell him I have had plenty of practice! We always laugh. He believes in me.

-Lisa Bass

Made in the USA
Columbia, SC
28 October 2024

44866472R00115